M000003929

PRAISE FOR

Christ's Basic Bodies

"This book gives us a compelling insight into the years of experience and knowledge of Dr Neighbour. His book reveals a man of much experience and profound maturity. I can recommend this persuasive work to every church leader and especially those in doubt and seeking direction. God has through the ages used people like Dr Neighbour to pioneer the changes that He wants for His *ekklesia*. I personally found this book profoundly insightful."
—*Harold F. Weitsz, Lead Pastor,*
Little Falls Christian Center, South Africa

"This book is another milestone in Ralph expressing what God is doing now in these last days – preparing the church for the completion of the Great Commission. When I read this book, I kept on saying "Amen" to what Ralph is saying. Basically, he is expressing what I have been receiving from God and His Word . . . and also what many others Christian leaders are receiving."
—*Ben Wong, Author and Coordinator,*
Cell Church Missions Network

"Ralph Neighbour is the 'guru' of cell church ministry. Best of all, Ralph models and lives the truths he knows so well. In this book, Ralph challenges us to go beyond structure, formula, and success in cell ministry and to remember what the cell is all about: Christ living through each group member. God challenged me through this book to remember that cell ministry is not a man-made enterprise (or means to church growth). It's all about Jesus! I'm sure that God will challenge and change you as you read Ralph's insight into the nature of the church. Thanks, Ralph, for helping us to refocus on Jesus."
—*Joel Comiskey, Ph.D.,*
Founder and President, Joel Comiskey Group

PRAISE FOR
Christ's Basic Bodies

"Ralph Neighbour for years has been espousing the way we should be doing church. He has been heard loudly and clearly across the world and deserves to be heard and read in this standard-bearing book. The strongest issue about this book is that he articulates what the church should look like in view of the eternal Kingdom of God. The loss of Kingdom mentality has been the church's costliest loss and I am delighted to say that God is in process of restoring the Kingdom to the Church. Few voices have sounded as clear a message to our confused religious culture as that of Ralph Neighbour regarding the church in this significant process. Read it carefully and take heed!"
—*Jack Taylor, President,*
Dimensions Ministries, Melbourne, Florida

"In the early 1990s, reading Ralph Neighbour's radical, confrontational books messed up everything I thought about ministry and changed my future ministry in the church. This book radicalizes the radical. It is the culmination of a radical's life-long reflection, experience, and experimentation with what it means to be Christ's bride. You may not agree with everything he writes, but you will have to wrestle with his challenges."
—*Scott Boren, Pastor, Author and Church Consultant*

"In this book, Dr. Neighbour explains two profound truths about the nature of the Church: The first is that the Church is the spiritual body on earth of the eternal and pre-existent Christ. The second is that the eternal and pre-existent Christ expresses Himself uniquely through the small group communities of the Church. Dr. Neighbour passionately makes the case that the small group is not just a method or a structure, but is the most basic spiritual life of the eternal and pre-existent Christ. He carefully explains how the Christ of Scripture expresses Himself in the practical life of small group community. This book of practical theology is necessary for those who wish to fulfill the mission of the Church to reach the 21st Century World."
—*Bill Beckham, Author and Cell Church Consultant*

PRAISE FOR
Christ's Basic Bodies

"Ralph Neighbour has crafted a well written book that, to my mind, is his best yet. Deeply Christ-centered and demonstrating a firm grasp of the inseparable union between Christ and His church, this book will give readers much to ponder. I would especially recommend this book to all who are part of missional and incarnational communities."
—*Frank Viola, Author*

Christ's Basic Bodies

Christ's Basic Bodies

Embracing God's presence,
power, and purposes in
true biblical community

Ralph W. Neighbour, Jr.

TOUCH Publications
Houston, Texas U.S.A.

Published by TOUCH Publications
P.O. Box 7847
Houston, Texas, 77270, U.S.A.
800-735-5865 • www.touchusa.org

Copyright © 2008 by Ralph W. Neighbour, Jr.

All rights reserved. No part of this publication may be
reproduced, stored in a retrieval system, or transmitted,
in any form or by any means, electronic, mechanical,
photocopying, recording, or otherwise, without the prior
written permission of the publisher. Printed in the United
States of America.

Cover design by Neubauer Design Group
Editorial Team: Scott Boren, Michael Mack,
Randall Neighbour, Matt Hammon, and Shae Cottar

International Standard Book Number: 978-0-9788779-8-9

All Scripture quotations, unless otherwise indicated,
are from the Holy Bible, New International Version,
Copyright © 1973, 1978, 1984 by International Bible
Society. Used by permission.

TOUCH Publications is the book-publishing division
of TOUCH Outreach Ministries, a resource and consulting
ministry for churches with a vision for a cell-based local
church structure.

Find us on the web at: http://www.touchusa.org

Discussion questions for each chapter can be found on the
author's blog: http://neighbourgrams.blogspot.com

Acknowledgements

Rick Yamamoto, a strategist for Mosaic in Los Angeles, thoughtfully read an early draft of this book and wrote, "For the most part, Generation X will probably just read the book and nod their heads in agreement. . . . You have a lot to offer the younger generation, and they would be interested if it was geared to their culture. Someone younger needs to read the manuscript to help you share the book to this audience."

So, I found two young bucks in ministry and asked them to review the manuscript. The current version is the result of suggestions made by Matt Hammon and Shae Cottar. Their input was invaluable to my writing process. Thank you both for your hard work and dedication to this project.

Finally, special thanks go to Randall Neighbour, my beloved son, who has poured over every sentence and greatly improved their structures. More important, he embodies the community life that is described in these chapters.

It is my desire to speak as a mentor to those who are trying to do something different. It is my prayer the chapters will be so used by our King, inspiring visionary young men and women to see the church not as it is, but as it can be.

Contents

Introduction 13

Section 1: Defining "Church"

1. Thinking Like God Thinks 23
2. Filters 33
3. Breaking Free From The Last Century 45
4. Body Parts —Proper Portions in Proper Places 57
5. The Size and Nature of Christ's Basic Bodies 91
6. Temple Furniture 109

Section 2: Theological Issues

7. The Community of the Godhead 125
8. The Four Tasks of the Eternal Christ 137
9. Christ Inhabits His Called-Out Ones 155
10. The Inseparable Bond 169

Section 3: Practical Issues

11. The Kingdom of God and Christ's Basic Bodies 181
12. How Are Christ's Basic Bodies Formed? 195
13. The "Energizings" — The Source and the Supplier 209
14. There's More, So Much More! 225
15. Here's The Baton — Will You Run With It? 241

End Notes 247

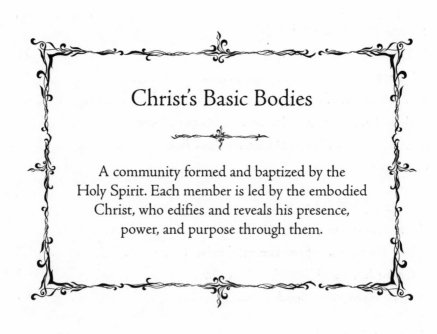

Christs Basic Bodies

A community formed and baptized by the
Holy Spirit. Each member is led by the embodied
Christ, who edifies and reveals his presence,
power, and purpose through them.

Introduction

After planting a dozen churches in the Northeast, working for Billy Graham, and serving on the Evangelism Division of the Baptist General Convention of Texas, I came to a moment of truth. The more I worked with churches large and small, the greater my frustration grew. Modern Christianity blockaded God's people in physical structures and the church no longer touched the people in the communities around them.

Dr. Penrose St. Amant was my professor at New Orleans Theological Seminary when I worked on a Th.D. in church history. He profoundly impacted me when he stated, "Those of you who get to this level of academics have a moral obligation to hold this denomination at arm's length and bring rebirth to it. This is your task!" That very day, God's Spirit impregnated my value system with those words and they shaped my journey.

I walked the floor in my Dallas home reflecting on my daily encounter with declining Baptist churches as I served them, praying about my destiny. At thirty-six years of age, I knew I had to respond to the burden in my heart. I thought, "Surely there is a way to help these churches renew their lifestyles and become more biblical in their structures."

I sensed the need for a "parable church" set in the midst of traditional structures. I did not desire to expose or criticize the traditional church. My hope was to lovingly show these churches a more effective way to reach people who would not be caught dead in a church building.[1]

I spoke to a professor of evangelism from Southern Seminary about my burden. He encouraged me to do something about it and assured me a biblical model would make an impact. I then wrote a sixty-eight-page strategy of what an "experimental church" might look like.

I decided the only way to begin would be to totally withdraw from organized church life or teach in a secular university to reach those whose paradigms had not been constrained by past experiences. With them, I would experiment with body life. I would affectionately keep my ties with my denomination, believing wholeheartedly that if I showed them a better way, they would respond with a passion to transition to a more life-giving environment and structure.

Correcting misconceptions

I have never been angry with my brothers and sisters in traditional structures, but I quickly admit my frustration with them . . . a frustration strong enough for me to sell all my security to buy the pearl of great price. At the time, Ruth, my precious wife, said, "Honey, if you know God is calling you to develop an experimental church, I'll return to nursing." My oldest son Ralph said, "Dad, I can get a job sacking groceries after school to help out." With three sons, a mother-in-law and two dogs to shelter and feed, I decided to make the break and do whatever it took to form a parable church.[2]

I have also never been "anti-church." Those in the old paradigm don't always have a framework for classifying me and so I am written off as "anti-church." This is simply not true. My passion has been the *restoration* of Christ's body, not the *assassination* of it. I am saddened by the frequent reference to me as the "father of the cell church movement." I have always advocated far more than this structural pattern for church life. My heartbeat is to help the church think how it lives its life, not just change its structures. Theology breeds its own methodology!

At seventy-nine, I know facts today that were fuzzy forty years ago. For example, in 1969, while launching our new lifestyle in the experimental church formed in Houston, I spoke at the Maryland Baptist Evangelism Conference. I shared with the executive secretary of a nearby state convention my dream of showing my love for the denomination by developing a prototype that could be a model for others. He pointedly said, "Ralph, no one asked you to do this. We do not need a new model. We are committed to make the present one work better!"

Ouch!

As the years have passed I realized he was telling me the truth. Denominations are imprisoned by their traditions. It takes a very special calling to be an innovator or early adopter. Power usually rests with the early and late majority and the laggards, not with the innovators and early adopters.

If I had to live my life over again, I would do exactly as I have done. I do not own a vision. *The vision owns me!* I pray, dear reader, that you will sense my love for the body of Christ as you read these pages. As Winston Churchill wrote, "If you have an important point to make, don't try to be subtle or clever. Use a pile driver. Hit the point once. Then come back and hit it again. Then hit it a third time—a tremendous whack."

This book is another whack at a message that is my life's calling and passion. It shouts, "*churchianity* blinds the people of God from being the body of Christ. God is reshaping the called-out people to live as Christ's bodies all over the earth!"

"Never ask a goldfish what water is like."

This Chinese proverb provides a metaphor for our church-structure dilemma. In this generation, the American church is a private goldfish bowl, now fully isolated from its surroundings. When fish stare into the glass walls of their bowl, they see only their mirrored reflection. They cannot see the world outside.

Churchianity is a goldfish bowl. Those who swim within it are unable to understand why their comfortable environment is not the only one needed. They are blind to how foreign they look to outsiders peering through the glass and murky water.

Have you ever thought about the fact that all living things are created to survive in a certain environment and will not survive if that environment is not proper? Consider fish. They experience only one environment: water. By their Creator, they are limited to exist in one habitat.

There is no reason for fish to reflect on the makeup of water. It's not an element to be analyzed, but rather an environment to be experienced. Within their environment, fish are sensitive to water conditions, all related to their own "comfort zones." They select a proper depth to provide the exact amount of light and heat to make them comfortable. They may experience dirty water, fresh water, or stagnant water, but to them it is always water and they don't have to give it much thought.

The contemporary church is a living thing, requiring a specific environment in which to survive and thrive. I believe it may be suffocating from the environment it currently inhabits without realizing it. For example, take the concept of the kingdom of God. "*Seek first his kingdom ... and all these things will be given to you as well*" (Matthew 6:33) is a familiar verse that is rarely pondered. It is time for kingdom people to select a lifestyle that has eternity in view rather than focusing on careers, sports, shopping, vacations, and TV specials.

A new term for a new season

After much prayer and contemplation, I am going to introduce a new word for referring to *ekklesia* in its most basic formation, sometimes called "cells" or "basic Christian communities" or "holistic small groups." I will use the term *Christ's Basic Body*. It defines what the contemporary church does not fully grasp: the authentic *ekklesia*[3] is not an opt-in small group. It is a spiritual body inhabited by Christ — answerable to him alone — empowered to reveal his presence, power, and purpose. As you will read repeatedly through this book, *it is the most sacred community on earth today*. We must remain diligent to fulfill the calling of *ekklesia*. (This term and the deeper meaning of it will be discussed in detail in chapters four and five.)

I beg of you: do not defensively reject what this book discusses until you have completed it. Please return with me to the source: Christ, the one who has chosen the *ekklesia* to be his body in this age. Ponder what is written. You may decide you are not a goldfish after all!

More than a decade ago I wrote *Where Do We Go from Here?* It introduced the cell church model to thousands of people. Since then, new Christ's basic bodies are found in great number on every continent.

Many versions of cell-based churches have appeared, each with their own oversight system. Far too much attention is paid to the management of cells compared to the awesome ecclesiology[4] that supports this "last days" church life. For this reason, I will deliberately not discuss church management systems in this book. The focus will remain far more foundational.

Many church-growth methods have become fads, endorsed by those who want to put patches on the old wineskin of traditional church life. Church leaders flock to conferences touting each new innovation, return excitedly from the seminars, read a book or two, and then idolize those patches. Some pastors even sever friendships with other workers over their loyalties to different patches. Soon enough, the old wineskin rots in another place and opens the way for another gimmick to be added as a patch. As you will see, I don't believe in patches. I do, however, believe that new wineskins can replace the old. Transition is taking place everywhere at this time.

I worked with hundreds of churches in South Africa in the mid 1990s. There was such a thirst for patches! The cell group structure was first seen as one more patch sewed on old structures. When pastors and churches adopted the goal to *replace* old wineskins, I helped pastors make the transition. For two years, I made quarterly trips back to walk them through a strategy to completely transform their congregations.

Today we have entered a third generation of the cell church

movement. Things are not the same as when my first book was written. Now there are many "streams." Some of these streams developed cell groups[4] as mere assembly lines to manufacture "converts" in rapid fashion. I am concerned they are growing mushroom groups that grow quickly but will not be able to survive the heat of spiritual warfare.

I believe the lethal ingredient at this stage is a fuzzy ecclesiology or an incomplete understanding of the sacredness of the body of Christ. It is to this issue I direct the chapters that follow. Please bear with me as I cover basic learning concepts before I move into the meat of the subject matter. The first chapter is vital to absorb to receive the balance of the book in a transformational way.

The gospel is hidden from those who are lost because the church has failed to live in biblical, holistic communities that clearly articulate their faith. Perhaps the greatest deterrent to the spread of the gospel is the existence of present "church" activity, which essentially focuses on what takes place in a building. Christ doesn't ask us to hold events for people to "come and see." We are challenged to go and be his body among the culture around us. I propose we reject this attractional model to embrace a more incarnational model. We must penetrate small, dark segments of society with the light of Christ's presence.

Our culture has had enough of the lifeless version of contemporary Christianity. The steady decline of church membership in America proves this. Only through Christ's basic bodies will we be able to bring the hope and life of the kingdom of God to an otherwise immune culture. Living in true biblical community provides flesh and blood to the words we speak. If we do not wake up to the problem, we will see more people lost from the kingdom of God.

I encourage you to read this book in small, bite-sized morsels, pausing to chew on the concepts before you move forward. As you read, please keep in mind the crucial issue of this book: *Christ indwells a sacred body, and we become its members as the Holy Spirit forms basic Christian communities!*

One final caveat: I strongly believe people fully absorb new information after they have heard it numerous times. My motto is: "It takes six to stick!" With this in mind, don't think this old man has forgotten what he said in an earlier chapter when concepts are revisited. The reprise is for your benefit. If you don't catch it the first time, maybe the second or third time it will sink in.

Are you ready? Shall we begin?

— Dr. Ralph W. Neighbour, Jr.

Defining "Church"

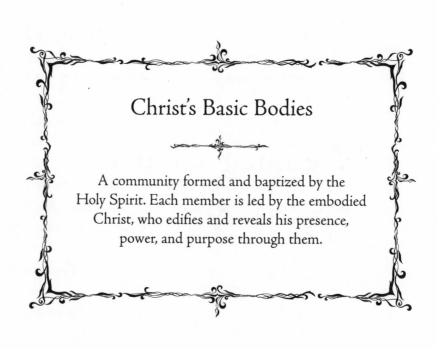

Christs Basic Bodies

A community formed and baptized by the
Holy Spirit. Each member is led by the embodied
Christ, who edifies and reveals his presence,
power, and purpose through them.

Thinking Like God Thinks

'For My thoughts are not your thoughts, nor are your ways My ways,' says the Lord. For as the heavens are higher than the earth, So are My ways higher than your ways, and My thoughts than your thoughts.

(Isaiah 55:8, 9, *NKJV*)

A man approached me and asked, "Will you pray for me so that my business will prosper? I am at the edge of bankruptcy and I need God to bless me."

I responded, "Let me ask you a question. Have you been faithful to honor God with the profits you made in the past? God said in Malachi that if we are faithful to him and do not rob him of his tithe, he will open the windows of heaven!"[1]

He admitted, "Well, I must say I have not supported the Lord's work for many years."

"I have a dilemma," I said, thinking aloud. "How do I ask God to bless a thief who has been stealing from God?"

Of course, that was not the end of our conversation. I went on to ask him if he thought a man should support his family as his first priority, and he agreed. I then asked him if he felt he belonged to a family of Christian people and that God wanted him to feel a responsibility to care for their needs? Just as most contemporary Christians would say, he stated: "I have never thought of my church as a family. As far as I can see, it's an organization."

The concept of life lived in community with fellow believers and the intimacy of family life among other believers had never dawned on him. He went on to explain that an invisible God who owned heaven and earth surely didn't need his few dollars. The Sunday program he attended twice a month was certainly not worth 10 percent of his earnings. According to this man, even a good movie—which was as long as an average church service—only costs eight bucks!

This man's core problem was that he considered tithing a legalistic demand to support a public institution. Nothing in his years of attending church meetings caused him to think he was part of a family that required financial support.

We must view life from God's perspective. That means rejecting the error that living the Christian life can be a self-centered activity. While Christ personally indwells "called-out ones" (*ekklesia*) among men, a fundamental act of the Holy Spirit is to sever us from our self-governing spirits and connect us to other members. This forms a body incarnated by Christ.[2] Living in community means you *"look not only to your own interests, but also to the interests of others."*[3]

Milt Rodriguez writes,

A good example of this corporate viewpoint can be seen in the earthly life of the Lord Jesus. He never worked alone. He spoke the words from the Father. He did the works of the Father. He cast out demons by the Spirit (Matthew 12:28). Jesus lived by the life of the Triune God. He could have lived alone and worked alone but that was not His choice. As a person, He has a will and the power to choose. And He chose, as a man, to live and work in the corporate life of God. He had a "corporate consciousness" and was aware of where He had come from. He was part of a Community and He was not going to act independently of that Community just because He was here on earth. In fact, the Father sent Him to continue that fellowship, that corporate lifestyle, here on earth so that His disciples would begin to "see" with new eyes. He wanted them to begin seeing from God's viewpoint.[4]

The prayer of Jesus was that believers might be one: *"Holy Father, protect them by the power of your name—the name you gave me—so that they may be one as we are one."*[5] How can that happen? We are separated by sex, age, language, culture, inclinations, moods, and occupations. Our present lifestyle as believers cannot begin to demonstrate what Christ had in mind for his new body.

The Son exists in the community of the Godhead. When he is present, the Father and the Spirit are fully present as well:

> *This is He who came by water and blood—Jesus Christ; not only by water, but by water and blood. And it is the Spirit who bears witness, because the Spirit is truth. For there are three that bear witness in heaven: the Father, the Word, and the Holy Spirit; and these three are one. And there are three that bear witness on earth: the Spirit, the water, and the blood; and these three agree as one.*[6]

When we have the Son, we have the fullness of the Godhead living within us: "these three are one." The mind of God for us is that *we* would be one.

God's perspective: we are to live in community

We must depart from a self-centered view of our life in Christ. We cannot independently remain apart from others. We are formed by the Spirit to be joined into community with others, forming a body indwelled by Christ.[7] As humans, we are always separate individuals, but it is never so in the kingdom of God. The life we have is one corporate body that expresses the life of the Son. We thus call God *our Father*.

Life in community begins with three people. Thus, God created each person to be physically born into community: "and baby makes three!" He also created the current body of Christ to begin when two or three are gathered in his name.[8] God then creates a community with a common activity, making it appropriate to see the members as a single body. They are given a special name in Scripture: "called-out ones" (*ekklesia*).[9] Note the term is plural, referring to a community, not individuals.

To fully unveil the nature of God, we must surrender our self-centeredness and "*look not only to [our] own interests, but also to the interests of others.*"[10] The essence of the triune God is best expressed when there is a God-made body to be viewed close-up.[11] The community of the Godhead must be made known by a special community incarnated by Christ. This is the task of the *ekklesia*. The community of the Godhead is never fully revealed through *organization*, but through an *organism*.

The understanding of that organism changes everything about our current practice of church life. Since the time of Constantine—all the way to the Reformation and through the previous century—the true nature of Christ's Basic Bodies has been missing.

The organic nature of Christ's Basic Bodies is expressed by the intimacy within the small group. It is a place "where everybody knows your name." It is a place where you can be seen and "seen through," where others are aware of your strengths and weaknesses. It is a place where others can rely on your strengths and support you when you falter. In this kingdom lifestyle, there are no lonely people. Moreover, Christ in the midst causes a level of love and spiritual power that sets it apart from all man-made structures.

That's what the struggling businessman I counseled had not experienced. He was out of touch with God because he was not in touch with what should have been his spiritual family.

Much of the Western church is impersonal. Believers gather to sit in rows, rarely caring who is hurting in the row behind them. Some percentage of the larger group gathers in small groups, but lack intimacy by endlessly discussing Bible passages, topics of interest, or performing a task for the bigger group's corporate gatherings. In church life today, only a small percentage of the total number of believers are aware of the indwelling presence and power of Christ.

Some churches are seeking to relate to the cultures of the unreached world, which is a giant step forward. They change their music to show they are not too "different." They make their public services more entertaining, but do not observe the indwelling Christ healing the sick, raising the dead, cleansing the leper, and setting captives free—unless it is a platform display of a single man's "anointing." However, they are not yet concerned that they do not reveal the supernatural presence and power of Christ to their own culture.

Contrast this with what I heard about a house church leader in China. He said to his group, "We have not seen anyone raised from the dead for five months! We must fast and pray!" The demonstration of Christ's power was the witness of the early *ekklesia*. Do we really believe *"Jesus Christ is the same yesterday and today and forever"*?[12] Should we not grieve that our words do not match our experience with the supernatural?

A graduate student from South India studied under me at Columbia International Seminary. He told me he was a church planter who started three to four new churches a year. When I asked him to describe his strategy for planting new work so rapidly, he replied, "I enter a village and I walk, fast, and pray for a few days. As I observe all the sick and lame and demon-possessed, I ask, 'Lord, who will you touch to reveal your presence in this place?' Then the Lord says, 'This one.' So I pray and deliver the person. Then the whole village is amazed and they come to hear me teach them. After a few weeks, the converts are established and I move on. It's a simple strategy, but it works!"

American believers do not realize how far short they have fallen from experiencing Christ's presence and power. The church cannot continue to embrace the present norms and trends of church life. As Manfred Haller has written, "We cannot cling to our present historical form of Christianity: it is not to be preserved or restored."[13]

In these last days,[14] the Godhead has thrust a unique community into the world. There is no single model to duplicate, no single pattern that can be mimicked as the sole "how to." The biblical form must be created by a radical new expression of *ekklesia*.

Christ's Basic Bodies are all formed by a single truth expressed in 1 Corinthians 12:12: *"For as the body is one and has many members, but all the members of that one body, being many, are one body, so also is Christ"* (NKJV). Paul uses the human body as an illustration. Looking at a human body, we see many members but only one person. He states clearly, *"so also is Christ."* Christ's presence in the world today must reveal the *community* of the Godhead. The important truth to be absorbed is simply that an authentic community is indwelled and empowered by Christ!

This is what makes Christ's Basic Bodies sacred. The image being left by today's church is that the size of the audience determines their success. Mass meetings are "blobs of protoplasm" with no evident body parts. The true body of Christ will first appear as the cell group reveals kingdom power, causing observers to fall on their faces saying, *"God is really among you!"*[15]

The significance of *oikos*

Scripture describes "household" by the Greek word *oikos*.[16] It always defines a small group of intimately related persons, small enough to allow maximum accountability to exist between them.[17] This may be seen as Christ's Basic Bodies because this term describes the basic building block of Christ's community on earth. These Basic Bodies do not exist independently. They are bound together to form a larger assembly of the *ekklesia*. Even as a single individual cannot reveal community, neither can a single Basic Body detach itself from fellow Basic Bodies and function independently.

Paul refers to this sacred *oikos* as a group where accountability and responsibility function. Christ is in the midst and controls the life of his body, empowering it. Each Basic Body can penetrate a small segment of society, revealing the presence and power of the indwelling Christ.

The birthplace of Christ's Basic Bodies: the cross

When was the bride of Christ born? Some Bible teachers say it happened at Pentecost. This is an inaccurate conclusion. The bride was birthed from the pierced side of Christ at Mount Calvary. Even as God created Adam's bride from his side, the second Adam gave birth to his new body, delivering her as his side was pierced and blood and water came forth. It is from the cross, even as he paid the penalty for all men's rejection of God's reign, that he gave birth to his new body, the *ekklesia*.

It was at Pentecost that the Spirit of Christ entered those who would compose his new body. Before it took place, the Holy Spirit had a work to do. Before there could be a true union of the new body members, they all had to be in "one accord." That took ten days of interacting in an upper room. A body could not be formed by arms and legs that would argue about being joined together. On this side of heaven, we will never know all that took place during those days in that upper room. But we do know that it brought them to unity.

In a most amazing event, the glory of the triune God entered 120 people gathered in total agreement.[18] The splinters of fire that fell upon each person were spiritual fire, not physical fire. It was the *Shekinah* fire,[19] the glory of God. It was the same *Shekinah* Moses observed in a burning bush that was not consumed by it.

Divine glory fell upon each person present. What was happening? Christ was returning to occupy his new body! The 120 experienced Christ incarnated in the body of Jesus. Now they would experience the presence of Christ indwelling their own bodies! His divine Spirit returned to occupy their human spirits.

They instantly realized his glory had indwelled them. With extreme emotion, they poured out into the streets crying, "Jesus Christ is back! He's back! He has come to live within us!" So overcome were they by the experience they were unaware the Holy Spirit was instantaneously translating their Galilean language into multiple languages spoken to those from different nations.[20] By the power of the Holy Spirit, the person of Christ had come to inhabit his new body.

Note that the mission of Christ was immediately activated through his new body. Jesus had instructed the group before he ascended into heaven to proclaim the news to all nations (*ethnos*). Within minutes of his entrance into their lives, they were doing exactly that. The first proclamation went to *"Parthians, Medes and Elamites; residents of Mesopotamia, Judea and Cappadocia, Pontus and Asia, Phrygia and Pamphylia, Egypt and the parts of Libya near Cyrene; visitors from Rome (both Jews and converts to Judaism); Cretans and Arabs"*[21] . . . all nations!

Indwelled by Christ, this new body has multiplied all over the earth, penetrating every nation. In his new bodily form, he reveals his presence through empowering their corporate life.[22] The mission of the new body of Christ is to be a proclamation not of *information*, but of revealing his *incarnation*.

Before the foundation of the earth, the Father planned the selection of those that would be part of Christ's habitation following his incarnation in the body of Jesus. His eternal plan had everything to do with his Son.

God did not come forth with a plan that was apart from his Son. The Father's plan was always only in Christ. The Father chose us in Christ before the world was even created.[23] God's good pleasure is to have many sons, predestined to be inhabited by his only begotten Son. It is by his Holy Spirit the sons are called out[24] and it is through the Holy Spirit we are guided into all truth.[25] Jesus Christ said of the Holy Spirit, *"He will bring glory to me by taking from what is mine and making it known to you."*[26]

So intimate is our identity with and in Christ that the book of Ephesians, chapter by chapter, positions us as seated with him in the heavenly realms[27] and positions him as incarnated in us on earth.[28] Together with him, we war against principalities and powers in the heavenly realms.[29]

VIEWING COMMUNITY
FROM GOD'S PERSPECTIVE

Let's look at this pivotal issue from the Father's point of view. If we will just say with Peter, *"You are the Christ, the Son of the living God,"*[30] the Lord will respond, *"this was not revealed to you by man, but by my Father in heaven."*[31]

But let's not stop there! From the viewpoint of the Father, Jesus went on to prophesy that he himself would become the rock upon which the *ekklesia* would be built.[32] He was making reference to his new incarnation and the way he would then, through this new body, provide his presence and power to bind and loose using the keys of the kingdom.

We must struggle with the filters that hinder us and deceive us about the true nature of Christ's Basic Body. The community is exclusively made up of *ekklesia*, "called-out ones," formed by the work of the Holy Spirit to receive the indwelling presence of Christ. What can be clearer than Paul's words in 1 Corinthians 12:27: *"Now you are the body of Christ, and each one of you is a part of it"*?

> *For this reason I kneel before the Father, from whom his whole family in heaven and on earth derives its name. I pray that out of his glorious riches he may strengthen you with power through his Spirit in your inner being, so that Christ may dwell in your hearts through faith. And I pray that you, being rooted and established in love, may have power, together with all the saints, to grasp how wide and long and high and deep is the love of Christ, and to know this love that surpasses knowledge—that you may be filled to the measure of all the fullness of God.* (Ephesians 3:14-19)

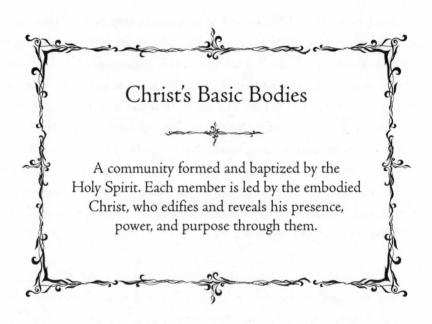

Christ's Basic Bodies

A community formed and baptized by the Holy Spirit. Each member is led by the embodied Christ, who edifies and reveals his presence, power, and purpose through them.

Filters

We don't yet see things clearly. We're squinting in a fog, peering through a mist. But it won't be long before the weather clears and the sun shines bright! We'll see it all then, see it all as clearly as God sees us, knowing him directly just as he knows us! But for right now, until that completeness, we have three things to do to lead us toward that consummation: Trust steadily in God, hope unswervingly, love extravagantly. And the best of the three is love.

(1 Corinthians 13:12, 13, *The Message*)

I know a man in Singapore who owns a business that sells filters. On a warehouse tour, he showed me filters for many applications. One filter screened out large stones. Another filter allowed only grains of sand to pass through. His company even sold coffee filters that allow only flavored water to seep into a pot.

As you pursue the balance of this book, you may discover you have personal filters that screen out new information that does not fit within your current paradigm. While I don't mind if you slam this book shut and "stew" over what you read in a given chapter, I do hope you will come back to it. If you can bypass your filter or current paradigm, we can continue our journey together.

On the other hand, as you read the following chapter, you may find that you have already gotten through or are in the process of moving through some of these filters. You're well on your way. As you dialogue with and take others through this journey, they will go through some of these stages. Perhaps the following information will help you lead them on this journey as you travel it together.

To begin, let's consider these comments by a respected colleague, William A. Beckham:[1]

During the last decade a new set of questions has been asked. These questions are not about the validity of using small groups but about the nature of such churches: what do they look like and how do they work? The House Church movement reacts against the failures of the large group and asks: "Is the large group necessary?" Another question arises because the most visible models for the movement to this point have been very large churches. "Is the small group strategy primarily a large church method?" However, a large percentage of churches in the world today are under 100 active adult members. Therefore, if the movement is to continue in the 21st Century, these small churches must energize the movement. And what is happening in China seems to prove that this is not just a large church phenomenon. Questions are being posed in other areas as well. How does church planting and support ministries fit into the movement?

Does a movement need to be controlled?

This is a question that has taken on great life over the past several years. The fact is the cell movement has lasted five decades with only the Holy Spirit as the divine administrator. It will not survive many more decades if human apostles tie it to themselves, box it into certain models, codify its life or forget to lead as servants. Leaders may be nouns or verbs. Noun leaders must have titles and positions. Verb leaders lead by example. Noun leaders say "Listen to me" and "Obey me." Verb leaders say: "Follow me" and "Let me serve you." A movement will not survive under leaders that demand titles and positions.

Do we seek man-made groups or God-made bodies of Christ?

The future of Christ's body will only continue as a New Testament movement when the groups are the Body of Christ and function as a basic Christian movement. The basic implementing unit of this movement must be God-made, Christ-indwelled and Spirit-empowered groups. The important issue is Christ. Does Christ show up in these groups as He promised? Is Christ in the midst of each group in divine presence, resurrection power and eternal purpose?

Will change continue in the 21st Century?

How successful will the transformation of the body of Christ be from this time forward? The continuation and effectiveness of this movement will be directly related to the answer to four questions:

+ Is the movement flowing out of the nature and heart of God?
+ Does the Holy Spirit control the movement?
+ Are Christians willing to die in order to live in community
  with Christ and each other?
+ Will the basic unit of this movement be God-made,
  Christ-indwelled and Spirit-empowered groups?

Ultimately, this movement is about God and how He expresses Himself as the Body of Christ on earth and how He empowers that Body through the Holy Spirit. As long as the movement is about Him, it will continue to be empowered:

May Christ shield me today against poison and fire,
Against drowning and wounding,
So that I may fulfill my mission and bear fruit in abundance.
Christ behind and before me, Christ below and above me,
Christ with me and in me, Christ around and about me.
Christ on my right and on my left,

Christ when I lie down at night, Christ when I rise in the
morning,
Christ in the heart of every man who thinks of me,
Christ in the mouth of everyone who speaks of me,
Christ in every eye that sees me, Christ in every ear that
hears me.   —St Patrick

Those of us who are stewards in the kingdom of God for this
generation are those who will shape the changes—but only as we listen
to the voice of the King! It is painful to think outside our habits and
traditions. It is more than detrimental, however, to stay within that
which is familiar and comfortable and not participate in the ongoing
work of Christ. Personal filters are the greatest enemy of change.

**FILTERS LEADING TO
CHARACTERIZATION**

UNAWARENESS
AWARENESS
WILLINGNESS
TO RECEIVE
CONTROLLED
ATTENTION
COMMITMENT

CHARACTERIZATION

As you read the following section
describing five filters that hinder the
adoption of change, consider which best
reflects your current paradigm for Christ's
Basic Bodies. When you determine which
filter you maintain, you have a choice to
make. Allow God to deal with the underlying
issue that has put that filter in place to
experience *characterization*, or hold it as a
place of safety.

Later, you should revisit this section to
better understand the filters maintained by
others. Each level reveals a level of commitment a person will make to a
new lifestyle that requires radical change. Note carefully what response
can be expected at each level and approach others with their filters in
mind to introduce change to them in a more effective way.

UNAWARENESS

This filter contains a screen so tightly woven that it does not allow new concepts to pass through. Imagine a thick piece of black plastic sheeting over the frame of a window. All sunlight and air is blocked from entering the room. With this filter in place, the person who lives in the room has no idea a window exists because it is so well covered.

The unawareness filter is maintained by *fear*. For example, traditional church program leaders who have worked very hard for their position may feel so threatened by change that they refuse to acknowledge its existence.

Those who possess the filter of unawareness cannot make a commitment to change or even consider the possibility of change. Their viewpoint for change of any sort is completely self-obstructed.

AWARENESS

When one possesses this filter, a new concept is *perceived* but not *received*. It is similar to a fixed screen on a window that allows sunlight and air to pass through. With this filter in place, the person who lives in the room looks through the screened window, but the screen remains a barrier.

The awareness filter is maintained by *concern*. If a person looks over his shoulder and sees disapproval in the eyes of his peers, the price of change will be too great. One does not change when man's benediction is more important than God's destination. The rich young ruler[2] was blocked by this filter. He was not about to sell all he had! Yet that is what we must do if we are to become an authentic bride of Christ.

Knowing an important truth does not require the adoption of it. Those with the filter of awareness could make a commitment to change, but will not do so.

WILLINGNESS TO RECEIVE

When one possesses this filter, a new concept is considered, but rarely adopted. It is illustrated best by describing a room with chicken wire over a window. A person living inside can reach out and touch what lies beyond the window to test it and see if it is worth the price of leaving the comfort of the room.

This filter is maintained by *self-doubt*. The person is unwilling to risk losing what he has, even if it is sub-standard. For example, some pastors see the dry rot of churchianity in their congregations, but have looming mortgage payments on a campus expansion. So, they refuse to implement necessary change unless it will increase giving. Or, a small group leader will refuse to permanently yield control of his group to Christ because he is afraid that "God won't show up" and he will look unprepared or foolish.

At this level, an individual may become inwardly restless, but the magnetic pull of safety and security limits his response. Change will be considered, however. Those with the filter of willingness to receive will consider change, but only one in ten will actually adopt it.

CONTROLLED ATTENTION

This is an elusive filter to self-diagnose because it is rife with deceit. Concepts are adopted, but a permanent shift in lifestyle has not occurred. Consider a room with open, unobstructed windows. A person living in this room sees great opportunity for change and reaches out to hold it at arm's length. He likes what he holds, but only finds it more valuable in his *mind* as a preferred place to live. He doesn't value change enough to crawl through the window and leave the room permanently. He works outside the window regularly, but returns to his room where he is comfortable.

This filter is maintained by a *reticence to take ownership*. For example, a pastor may read dozens of books about church renewal and maintain the ideal of "the priesthood of all believers." Yet he only experiments with cell groups or recommends them as one option among many for church involvement.

Years ago, I was deceived into thinking that when I moved church members to this level I had succeeded. The people faithfully followed me into a new lifestyle of ministry to others because they respected my leadership. However, their traditional values were not changed. When I left the church and a new pastor replaced me, everything I had taught and trained them to do collapsed like a house of cards. Their attitude was, "The king is dead; long live the new king!"

At this level of commitment, only 2 in 10 maintain any intention of becoming emotionally or spiritually involved in a radical change in ministry.

COMMITMENT

The commitment filter is often overridden by new obligations, tasks, or opportunities. Consider a person who left the safety of his windowed room to attend college. While there, he is fully committed to learning all he can. However, in the back of his mind, he knows he will graduate and move on to the next stage in life. Knowing so much more about rooms and living spaces, he will not return to the first room. He'll find a different room to inhabit with bigger windows, vaulted ceilings, and built-in bookcases.

This filter is maintained by *potential discouragement*. It is entirely possible for some to commit to a new structure, get everything organized, bleed a little from bumping into thorny issues, and decide it's not worth it. They will then jump to another innovation.

A dear lady who knows me well made me a little plaque using stained glass that now sits on my office windowsill. It has two letters: "D" and "Q." When I asked her what it meant, she said, "Ralph, it speaks to your greatest weakness: 'Don't Quit!'"

At this level, 8 people out of 10 who are active in church life participate as conditions allow. If the conditions change, their commitment will cease.

CHARACTERIZATION

Characterization is the condition of living without any filters. It's actually a filter in reverse. Everything a person of characterization sees is filtered through his vision.

It is no longer an outside activity and there is no room in which to return. The vision is inside the person and drives them to action.

With characterization, the change in paradigm and lifestyle filters out anything and everything that might hinder you from fulfilling the call of God on your life. You no longer own a vision; the vision owns you! You don't even *think* about the consequences of what you have committed to do and to become. Paul showed he was without filters and characterized by his ministry when he was warned of terrible consequences. He replied,

> But none of these things move me; nor do I count my life dear to myself, so that I may finish my race with joy, and the ministry which I received from the Lord Jesus, to testify to the gospel of the grace of God.[3]

What you will learn in the following chapters will take you out of an environment you have considered "normal" for church life. It is time to look at the life of the virtuous, fertile bride of Christ and realize why we cannot remain in the organized church as it exists. While it is possible to transition from it, I do not see the hope of preserving it or patching it.

A solemn thought for Christian workers

In his brilliant book, *The Structure of Scientific Revolutions,* Thomas Kuhn writes:

> Almost always the men who achieve these fundamental inventions of a new paradigm have been either very young or very new to the field whose paradigm they change . . . these are the men who, being little committed by prior practice to the traditional rules . . . are particularly likely to see that these rules no longer define a playable game and to conceive another set that can replace them.[4]

Change and new paradigms threaten only those whose comfortable positions might be eliminated. In 1937, Chester Carlson was a law student frustrated with the tedium of making copies of documents using a typewriter. He devised a way to do it using electrostatic energy. He took it to IBM, the U.S. Navy, and Kodak. All of their experts filtered his proposal and flatly rejected the idea. After all, what could black powder, a metal sheet, and a light produce that could replace photography? In 1950, Carlson finally found enough backing to create what would eventually be known as the Xerox Corporation. I can only imagine the established, long-term executives at IBM and Kodak shook their heads in self-disgust when Xerox changed the business landscape.

In my thirties, God led me to make a huge paradigm shift. Are you willing to shed your filters to make one as well?

Filters are much like chicken pox. As a child, you knew *when* you contracted the disease, but you may not know *who* passed along the virus. I have examined my own filters to find their origin, process the thinking behind those filters, and moved. As you read my story, consider your own filters: when and where were you when you formed your current views about the body of Christ?

My pilgrimage toward characterization

Growing up in a pastor's home gave me a view of "church" that focused on sermons, Sunday School, buildings with organs and pews, and being a good boy so as not to disgrace my Dad or harm his reputation. I was totally *unaware* of the true nature of Christ's body. I swam like a goldfish in that bowl called a sanctuary, going from one meeting to the next, sitting on the front row beside my mother.

Awareness broke through as I realized God was more than a word. Hurlburt's Bible Stories exposed me to the many events where God dealt with Adam, Abraham, David, Goliath, and dozens of others. "Church" became a place I went to hear stories about God and men.

Willingness to receive church life came when I realized that if I were baptized I could take communion with the grownups. My "profession of faith" was as sincere as a child's could be, whose mind did not think in abstracts.

Controlled attention developed further concepts within me concerning "church" as a lifestyle. I watched my dad wrestle with church politics in a religious organization controlled by wealthy businessmen. This filter, along with the others I adopted, screened out any comprehension of community or a Christ-directed life. As a teen, I prepared to take my place as a preacher and teacher of the scripture, excited by the opportunity to proclaim the gospel message. My awareness of salvation's dimensions were well established by this time, but my awareness of a body of people inhabited by the Son of God was totally missing.

As I grew in education and experience, I was exposed to all the mechanics and structures of organized Christianity. My paradigm could almost be likened to a wire cage that limited my lifestyle. Using all my skills and talents, majoring in speech and drama, I devoted my full attention to being a "success" as a Christian worker.

The stage of *Commitment* placed me in the 75-hour work week of a devoted "man of God" who had to win the world at all costs. In a matter of a few years, many churches had been planted in large areas of Pennsylvania, New Jersey and New York. I slept in my car because I could not afford a motel. The Keystone Baptist Association was formed as a result of being committed.

It was at this point my paradigm began to become my enemy. I began to look "outside" the parameters of church as an organization rather than an organism. Reading the book of Acts and Paul's comments about the *ekklesia* being the literal body of Christ finally destroyed the last remnants of the cage in which I lived.

Characterization meant a break with all the "busy work" of organizing the church. It provided the liberating awareness that Christ dwelled in me and the members of His authentic body. That growing *awareness* led to *willingness to receive*, to *controlled attention*, to a new *commitment* to a radical, beautiful lifestyle lived in community. Finally, I discovered there was nothing better or more powerful to override my commitment to life in Christ's Basic Bodies.

It is my earnest prayer that this book will lead you out of old paradigms to lay hold on the authentic church, the last days event the Holy Spirit is now shaping by placing Christ in the living center of His new body.

He who has an ear, let him hear what the Spirit says to the ekklesia.
(Revelation 2:7)

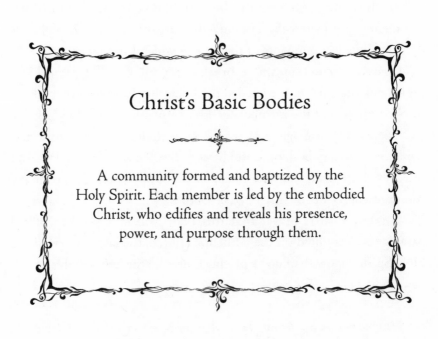

Christ's Basic Bodies

A community formed and baptized by the
Holy Spirit. Each member is led by the embodied
Christ, who edifies and reveals his presence,
power, and purpose through them.

c h a p t e r   t h r e e

Breaking Free
From The Last Century

*Not that I have already obtained all this, or have already been made perfect,
but I press on to take hold of that for which Christ Jesus took hold of me.
Brothers, I do not consider myself yet to have taken hold of it. But one thing
I do: Forgetting what is behind and straining toward what is ahead, I press
on toward the goal to win the prize for which God has called me heavenward
in Christ Jesus. All of us who are mature should take such a view of things.
And if on some point you think differently, that too God will make clear to
you. Only let us live up to what we have already attained.*

(Philippians 3:12-16)

Many changes took place in church life in the last century.
Evangelicals would be impacted for many generations by the life of
Dwight L. Moody (1837-1899). His evangelistic crusades placed one
hand on England and another hand on America and pushed both under
the shadow of the cross. Evangelistic crusades, large and small, featuring
such men as Sam Jones, R. A. Torrey, Billy Sunday, Billy Graham, and
Bill Bright continued this. I have met dozens of converts from the
crusades held by my own grandfather, R. E. Neighbour, who conducted
months-long campaigns in cities all over America.

It was obvious that the century would produce an explosion of new
believers all over the earth. Missionaries were disbursed in greater and
greater numbers to distant lands, penetrating new people groups with
great passion. New martyrs were added to those of earlier centuries,
including my own classmates: Jim Elliott, Nate Saint, Roger Youderian,
Pete Fleming, and Ed McCulley.

Even non-Charismatic believers must respect the changes in church life caused by the Azusa Street Revival of 1906-1915.[1] What began with a humble movement in Los Angeles, California, brought a tidal wave of change to Christianity for a century. Some think the impact is among the most significant events since the time of the Reformers.

That event is referred to as the "First Wave." It rolled over Christianity as a tsunami. One special theology was forever impacted—the place of the Holy Spirit in the personal experience of believers.

New denominations came into existence as the new term "Pentecostal" was used. South Africa was so impacted by the ministry of John G. Lake[2] following his experience at Azusa Street that the Apostolic Faith Mission (AFM), now two million strong, became the rival of the strongly entrenched Dutch Reformed Church. The AFM members were so zealous that the national railway system (controlled by dignitaries in the Dutch Reformed Church) deliberately transferred employees who were members of the AFM to remote villages at the "end of the lines" to limit their influence in the cities.[3] Of course, this move backfired and resulted in the planting of hundreds of new AFM churches!

Around the world, the new theology formed new Pentecostal seminaries. These institutions trained pastors to add new wine into the old wineskins patterned after Reformation-period church structures. The phenomenon fragmented most Protestant and many Roman Catholic churches in unprecedented ways.

New conflicts began as the Charismatic wave rolled in. This "Second Wave" hit the shores of traditional church life and formed a new group of parachurch structures catering to those who could not find the new wine in their churches. Women were "aglow" and business men met for lunches, separated from church life.

Then came the "Third Wave."[4] Signs and wonders classes at Fuller Theological Seminary launched still another high tide on the beaches. Another batch of denominations arose focusing on healing and spiritual gifts. John Wimber became one of the apostles of the movement. His Vineyard churches formed "kinship groups" that met essentially for fellowship, committed to following the Holy Spirit's empowerment.

At this same time, some Evangelicals gathered around a "Fullness Movement," not wishing to be labeled as Pentecostal or Charismatic, yet proclaiming the Holy Spirit's power within. It was not really a "Fourth Wave," and for the most part receded as the tide went out.

Running parallel to these events, dozens of large, global parachurch structures emerged. Theological differences created evangelistic movements such as Youth for Christ, Youth with a Mission, Campus Crusade, and Young Life. Others, like The Navigators, became strong in a discipleship focus. Bible Study Fellowship, Focus on the Family, and similar organizations sprang up to enhance, but may have become competitive with local churches. Each provided separate outlets for Christian living and focused on a particular area of expertise. Some attempted to influence congregations. Others concluded local churches were fruitless structures and raided them for staff and funds.

Another "side structure" was Promise Keepers, which gathered men from local churches, along with their pastors, into huge stadiums. Reaching into the prison system took on a new focus through Chuck Colson; more than twenty-nine new prison ministries followed, still active in America today.

Sadly, the need for a new wineskin was hidden from view. Few realized the true body of Christ would require the Holy Spirit to form Christ's Basic Bodies. Thus, the tide of the Holy Spirit's activity hit the beaches, but never transformed building-centered, program-focused, clergy-led church forms.

A new theology of the Holy Spirit

As I stated earlier, the *personal* baptism of the Holy Spirit thus became the primary focus. The baptism of groups by the Holy Spirit, joined believers as Christ's basic body, was a total blind spot.

A full connection was never made to join individuals together, sent to dwell as his community and to do his work.

This passion of the Azusa movement failed to embrace the importance of Christ's position as the Head of the community (*ekklesia*[5]). Consider the words of Frank Bartleman, one of the key personalities in the 1906 Azusa Street movement. (Some call him "the father of the Pentecostal Movement.") Concerning this issue, he wrote:

> In the beginning of the Pentecostal work, I became very much exercised in the Spirit that Jesus should not be slighted, "lost in the temple," by the exaltation of the Holy Spirit and of the gifts of the Spirit. There seemed to be a great danger of losing sight of the fact that Jesus was "all, and in all." I endeavored to keep Him as the central theme and figure before the people. Jesus will always be the center of our preaching. All comes through and in Him. The Holy Spirit is given to "show the things of Christ."
>
> The work of Calvary, the atonement, must become the center of our consideration. The Holy Spirit never draws our attention from Christ to Himself, but rather reveals Christ in a fuller way. We are in the same danger today.
>
> There is nothing deeper nor higher than to know Christ. Everything is given by God to that end. The "one Spirit" is given to that end. Christ is our salvation and our all. That we might know "the breadth, and length, and depth, and height of the love of Christ" (Ephesians 3:18-19), having a "spirit of wisdom and revelation in the knowledge of Him" (Ephesians 1:17). It was "to know Him (Christ)," for which Paul strove.
>
> I was led to suddenly present Jesus one night to the congregation at Eighth and Maple. They had been forgetting Him in their exaltation of the Holy Spirit and the gifts. Now I introduced Christ for their consideration. They were taken completely by surprise and convicted in a moment. God made

me do it. Then they saw their mistake and danger. I was preaching Christ one night at this time, setting Him before them in His proper place, when the Spirit so witnessed of His pleasure that *I was overpowered by His presence, falling helplessly to the floor under a mighty revelation of Jesus to my soul.* I fell like John on the Isle of Patmos, at His feet.

I wrote a tract at this time, of which the following are extracts: "We may not even hold a doctrine, or seek an experience, except in Christ. Many are willing to seek power from every battery they can lay their hands on in order to perform miracles, draw the attention and adoration of the people to themselves, thus robbing Christ of His glory and making a fair showing in the flesh. The greatest religious need of our day would seem to be that of true followers of the meek and lowly Jesus. Religious enthusiasm easily goes to seed. The human spirit so predominates the show-off, religious spirit. But we must stick to our text—Christ. He alone can save.

The attention of the people must be first of all, and always, held to Him. A true 'Pentecost' will produce a mighty conviction for sin, a turning to God. False manifestations produce only excitement and wonder. Sin and self-life will not materially suffer from these. We must get what our conviction calls for. Believe in your own heart's hunger and go ahead with God. Don't allow the devil to rob you of a real 'Pentecost.' Any work that exalts the Holy Spirit or the gifts above Jesus will finally end up in fanaticism. Whatever causes us to exalt and love Jesus is well and safe. The reverse will ruin all. The Holy Spirit is a great light, but will always be focused on Jesus for His revealing."[6]

When the Pentecostal movement did not experience life lived in fellowship with the indwelling Christ, the artesian river that flows from him as the life source was lost. Christ stated, *"Whoever believes in me, as the Scripture has said, streams of living water will flow from within him."*[7] The fountainhead of the rivers is the indwelling Christ. The flowing of those rivers is the ministry of the Spirit.[8]

Unfortunately, what Bartleman sought to correct did not change what happened in the evolution of the first wave. In spite of this oversight, God allowed this wave, using their passion to shake the foundations of the intellectual focus of the 1800s. The wave pointed out the place of *experience* as critical to kingdom living. Yet, even today, some vehemently insist, "Jesus is in heaven, seated at the right hand of the Father. It is the Holy Spirit that works in our generation."

By midcentury, the new theology of the Holy Spirit had become so popular that new ministries emerged around personalities. Men like Oral Roberts attracted the masses to view miracles displayed "on stage." Platform "manifestations" played well on the growing Christian television networks. As a result, many Christians now function individually and "worship God" at home by viewing their favorite preachers on TV.

A report by George Barna reflects the results of this. His organization's latest study identifies a growing trend for spiritual Americans to exercise their faith in places other than church buildings. Moreover, Barna commented that he would not be surprised if a larger portion of the born-again population shifts "from the 'churched' to 'unchurched' column of the ledger over the next 10 years."

Barna found that one out of five unchurched people read the Bible in a typical week, six out of ten pray to God each week, and one out of twenty have shared their faith in Jesus Christ with people who are not professing Christians during the past year. Also, nearly one million unchurched adults tithe their income, though the money typically goes to a variety of parachurch ministries rather than to a local church.

During a typical month, six out of ten unchurched adults worship God in a place other than a church service, Barna said. Three out of ten study the Bible and one out of seven has times of prayer and Bible reading with family members. Four out of ten seek Christian enrichment through television, radio, magazines, or faith-based websites, and one-fourth of unchurched adults claim to have conversations with one or more friends who hold them accountable for carrying out their faith principles.

Overall, Barna concluded that one in three American adults are unchurched. "To view the plateaued level of the unchurched population as simply an indication of stagnation in religious behavior is naive," Barna said. "There are, indeed, millions of unchurched people who want nothing to do with organized religion or spiritual development. The more important trend, however, is that a large and growing number of Americans who avoid congregational contact are not rejecting Christianity as much as they are shifting how they interact with God and people in a strategic effort to have a more fulfilling spiritual life."[9]

It's time for a move to the next level. We must pray every day that God will increase our anointing and make better use of us. Charles Carrin has stated, "The peak of church life is not found in where we have been. It is in the future. We must press toward the point where the power of the Holy Spirit will become the strongest. Unless we will press into God, we will never reach that final destination."

The moment we think we have "arrived," we will miss the "more." R. T. Kendall has said,

In 1992 the first Word/Spirit Conference in England that I know of was at Wembley Conference Centre in London, and I gave an address that got me into more trouble than any message I have ever, ever brought in my whole life, in which I made this statement: that as Abraham sincerely thought that Ishmael was the promised son—you remember the story—how he had been given the promise of a son and then, as he was getting older, no son was coming, and so Sarah said to Abraham, 'Sleep with my servant Hagar,' and he did, and Ishmael was born. For thirteen years Abraham was happy, that was the way God was going to do it. One day God said to Abraham, "Wrong! Ishmael is not it. Isaac is coming!" The very thing that Abraham once wanted, that a son should come through Sarah, he now was saying, "Oh, no!"

There are a lot of people who, because their appetites change, and things change, the very thing that they once wanted, now when it is offered them, they say, "Oh, no!" I remember putting a word to a charismatic leader in Britain back in 1992, I said, "Do you believe the Charismatic Movement is 'IT,' that it is the ultimate, that it is the fulfillment of all that we've hoped for?" How would you feel if the Charismatic Movement is Ishmael, and that Isaac is coming?" It distressed him.

That night, in the Wembley Conference Center, I preached a message that said all we've seen up to now is Ishmael. I offended more Charismatics and Pentecostals and also Evangelicals, because I said, "Any church worth its salt in Britain is usually charismatic, because churches are dying right, left, and center in Britain. So I've come to announce that Isaac is coming! As the promise of Isaac is so much greater than what happened with Ishmael, so what is coming is proportionately greater than anything we have ever seen, and I for one happen to believe we're 'that close to it.' There's more!"[10]

That future "more" connects to Christ's presence and power being restored to its central place in God's eternal plan. Since 1905 there has been an overstress on the place of the Holy Spirit and a reduction of the role of Christ in the strategy of God to establish his kingdom on the earth. The crucial place of Christ's new body composed of basic Christian communities was invisible to nearly everyone. This centrality must be restored!

To summarize, the Azusa Street movement failed to see the *ekklesia* as Christ's body, the basic Christian community. Swaddled in the grave clothes of Reformation church traditions, this new Holy Spirit theology was poured into old wineskins. The new Pentecostal denominations duplicated the old structures of the Reformers. New names like "Assemblies of God" did not reform building-centered, clergy-centered patterns. The new assemblies were still "large wing."[11] The wineskin did not change with the new wine inserted! They inherited the same structures as their non-Pentecostal neighbors and built organizations similar to them.

Karen Hurston has commented, "My perspective is this: God only gives us what we can take. Many of the 'phases' we have gone through were 'seasons' that have led us to the current season—and we need to honor each past season in order to embrace the greater truth of the new season God wants to bring."[12]

God cannot be properly discerned apart from life in community. However, the movements of the last century failed to grasp the importance of the "last days" wineskin, the basic Christian community, or Christ's Basic Body.

Self-shaping spirits emphasized that each individual must receive a personal baptism in the Holy Spirit to the exclusion of shared life as body members. A century has now passed as teachers have expounded on how this exposure to a single part of the Godhead—the Holy Spirit—would be the final answer. In reality, *there's more*. When one is baptized he is not just baptized by the Holy Spirit, he is baptized into the body of Christ—the family of believers that, together, continue Christ's work and carry his identity.

Two flaws in the three "waves"

From the human side, the new teaching did not discern the sacredness of the body of Christ. From the divine side, one part of the Godhead, the Holy Spirit, became the dominant focus. This also led to the heresy of the "Jesus only" theology among Pentecostals that rejected the Trinity—another aberration of rejecting the significance of Colossians 2:9, 10.[13]

As mentioned above, the new movement attracted a plethora of independent personalities, all appearing as "prophets" and "apostles." Some became faith healers with tents who created mayhem with cultish teachings. For example, William Branham, endorsed by Kenneth Hagin as a "prophet,"[14] taught that the Word of God was given in three forms: the zodiac, the Egyptian pyramids, and the written Scripture![15] He denied the Trinity, calling it a "doctrine of the devil."[16] Experience-based abuses became signs that "the Spirit has come."

Radio preachers offered "anointed cloths" for a contribution to the ministry that could be rubbed on a sick part of the body for healing. Trips to the Holy Land were made with piles of letters transported from the viewing audience so holy hands could be laid on them in front of the empty tomb of Jesus. Television programs now show mass audiences in hysteria, creating bewilderment among non-Christians who wonder how gullible Christians can become.

Thus, as the "wave" of the new emphasis on the centrality of the Holy Spirit emerged from Azusa Street, the tsunami soon included trash. Our task today is to somehow reclaim the reality from the foreign substances. We must break free from the mayhem and remain solidly committed to the reality found in these waves.

The debris in the water was observed very early in the last century:

> Seymour came preaching a new Pentecostal message: Speaking in tongues was the "Bible evidence" of being baptized in the Spirit, just as it was in the beginning in the book of Acts. This Seymour argued, is a recovery of New Testament Christianity. . . . Seymour preached a vision of racial equality where "the color line is washed away in the blood." . . . Sadly, this passion for love and unity among the races was eventually overwhelmed by the

entrenched racism of American culture in the early 20th century. Seymour would be deeply hurt by this. . . . As he observed the racial bigotry of those who claimed to have been baptized in the Holy Spirit, with tongues-speech as proof, he gradually adjusted his view on "Bible evidence," putting the emphasis on the fruit of the Spirit as the most important evidence that one was Spirit-filled.

He would still believe speaking in tongues was a genuine and significant gift from God, one that could be a sign of the Spirit's empowering, but not *the* sign. . . . Seymour believed that the baptism of the Holy Spirit should have an ethical impact on the lives of those who received it. In his mind, those who persisted in racism or other sins were not necessarily Spirit-filled just because they spoke in tongues. . . . Seymour . . . saw Spirit baptism as coming with a purpose, a "commission." It was an experience that empowered the believer to be a more effective witness for the gospel, and speaking in tongues was more than a "badge" verifying the reception of the Spirit . . . [it] was fundamentally an anointing from God to evangelize a world in need of Christ.[17]

Is it possible in this new century that there is more? It is time to absorb the valid parts of Pentecostal theology and cast out the trappings of extremes. Yes, there is more! God is at work in our world.

By holding on to the good in the Pentecostal expression while refocusing ourselves with Christ as the center, we discover how the Holy Spirit enables us to live as Christ's Basic Bodies. As Seymour learned, the true *charisma* is the life lived fulfilling our role as an extension of the presence of Christ, not just as separate individuals on our own mission. This life is lived by the empowering of the Holy Spirit who is the "one called alongside to help" Christ and ourselves, the one who approaches him on our behalf making "groans that words cannot express," bringing from him the many grace gifts he will manifest through us to repair others.

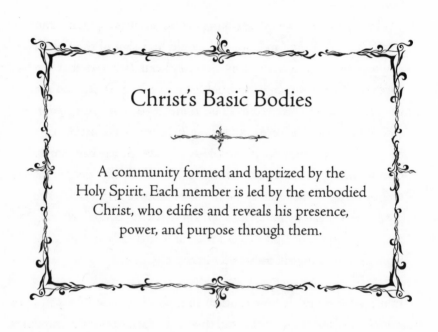

Christ's Basic Bodies

A community formed and baptized by the
Holy Spirit. Each member is led by the embodied
Christ, who edifies and reveals his presence,
power, and purpose through them.

Body Parts
Proper Portions in Proper Places

What we have is one body with many parts, each its proper size and in its proper place. No part is important on its own.

(1 Corinthians 12:20, *The Message*)

The body we're talking about is Christ's body of chosen people. Each of us finds our meaning and function as a part of his body . . . So since we find ourselves fashioned into all these excellently formed and marvelously functioning parts in Christ's [basic] body, let's just go ahead and be what we were made to be, without enviously or pridefully comparing ourselves with each other, or trying to be something we aren't. (Romans 12:5, 6, *The Message*)

The Holy Spirit is restructuring Christ's Basic Body for his present assignment: the discipling of all nations

This book is about the nature of what we call "church." For centuries, this word has created mental images: buildings, meetings, programs, structured designs for religious interaction, and so forth. We have not valued people and communal living. Instead, the emphasis has been on numbers, fame, and reputations. We now live in a period when "celebrity Christianity" allows men to use their own names to define the "church" people attend. The term is further confused by television program hosts who use the word "church" to include viewers at home. One observer has suggested the largest church attendance today is found in bedrooms across America. He calls it the "Church of Warm Springs!"

We need a new term that defines "church" as a reference to a small community of believers. Back in the 1970s, the term "cell" was used to define small groups who reveal the indwelling Christ to unbelievers. Before I found the word, I vowed to plant an experimental church that would find a more biblical lifestyle for Christians. While interviewing Dr. Donald McGavran, he told me to go visit the church pastored by Yonggi Cho in Seoul, Korea. Like dozens of others who went to see what was happening, I saw an awesome community of devoted believers who met in cell groups. His book, written at that time, seems to be the means of the word "cell" becoming universal in defining "church."[1]

The word defined a basic life form! Christ's body, made up of hands, feet, and inward parts would all be energized by him to manifest spiritual gifts. Finally, I thought, Christ's body will hear his voice and demonstrate his kingdom activity while unbelievers observe with amazement!

To encourage the use of this new word defining "church," TOUCH Outreach Ministries was established. The goal was to prepare American Christian workers to form *cell groups* (church) to reveal the indwelling Christ to unbelievers.[2] Our goal was not to create a pseudo-denomination, but to prepare existing churches for transitioning to a new lifestyle. Seminars and publications focused on the training and ministry of this new format.

As we were casting a vision for what a cell church could achieve for the kingdom, many eager and innovative types of pastors returned to their pulpits determined to become change agents. Sadly, few of them had any authority to make such radical change. Soon enough, my home phone rang late at night, and I listened to the story of yet another pastor who had just been sacked by church leaders who stubbornly refused to accept the new lifestyle. I despaired of seeing cell churches work in America!

I then wrote *Where Do We Go From Here?* as a "parting shot" to the American church, declaring it would not work in a nation spoiled by "churchianity." Just before it was published, I accepted an invitation to go back to Singapore to work with a new work, led by those who were open to forming and refining a cell-based structure.

With Christ in the school of transitioning core values

I learned much more about how a cell church should operate by moving to Singapore in 1990. I invested five years carefully implementing cells during my second time to serve in this island city. The first time was from 1975-1977. In the 70s, this tiny nation contained only a two percent Christian population. Youth for Christ was working among high school students. As I worked part-time with them, sharing the gospel under trees with teens, we experienced hundreds of decisions. These were young "closet" believers, teens afraid to announce to their Buddhist parents their commitment. An angry father broke the arm of his fifteen-year-old daughter after she told her parents she had decided to follow Christ! Thus these youth remained "underground" until they became adults.

When I returned in 1990, I found a miracle . . . hundreds of young believers were entering young adulthood, unspoiled by western church traditions. They came "out of the closet" in huge numbers, zealously announcing their faith in Christ. By 1995, we helped thousands form cell groups. The church even had a bulletin board with changeable numbers on the wall of the church office that was revised daily, reporting conversions phoned in from cell members and leaders.

Then in 1994 Apartheid was finally abolished in South Africa. Because of this social disease, their churches had been isolated from the rest of the world since 1948. A pastor who came to visit us in Singapore arranged for me to speak in seven different locations to explain the cell church theology and methodology. The response was awesome! Thousands came to the three-day presentations and instantly accepted the new vision for church life.

Knowing that transitioning a church would require several years of transforming core values, I was alarmed when I discovered many pastors returned to their churches and made *instant* changes to their structures. Three days of teaching was simply inadequate to prepare pastors for the changes they would have to make. It was then that I developed a series of weeklong seminars for church leaders called "The Year of Transition." I feverishly wrote the content in Houston and returned every three months for two years to train pastors who gathered for seminars in Cape Town, Durban, and Johannesburg.

The training focused on the premise that "theology breeds methodology!" (Remember, by "theology" I concentrated on only one area: their *ecclesiology,*[3] or the doctrine related to the structure of "church.") While suggestions were given about ways to structure a cell *meeting*, the primary focus was on redefining the word "church." Christ dwelling in small groups formed to be his body were to become "basic Christian communities" (what I now call Christ's Basic Bodies).

Sadly, the *theology* was ignored by many of the South African pastors. Most adopted the *methodology* without the theology. The importance of developing core values before creating structures was often ignored. Without a proper understanding that the cells were bodies inhabited by Christ, some strayed far from a New Testament model.

Thus, "cells" often became whatever their church leaders chose to make them. Instead of demonstrating how Christ expresses himself by empowering the life of his body, these groups became exclusive and ingrown. Sometimes, the members sat isolated in organized circles until they became bored and faded away. (We now know the average life of such groups is five years or less.)

My son Randall recently visited an African nation to meet with pastors who had traveled down to South Africa in 1996 for my training. They took the methodology home *without* the theology. Randall was shocked to see how far their "cells" had departed from the reality of true body life. What these precious pastors are calling "cells" are only small gatherings where the leader lectures and the members listen. Sadly, they struggle to engage with the unbelievers around them.

Of course, there are many notable exceptions in the present cell movement. The *Eglise Protestante Baptiste Oevres et Mission* in the Ivory Coast has grown to 190,000 members, all in Christ's Basic Bodies. Elim has gathered tens of thousands in the groups in El Salvador and other nations. Notable in South Africa is the Little Falls Christian Centre in Roodeport, planting a new congregation of cell groups every month. The Revival Centre in Blomfontain now numbers well more than 60,000 believers, with cell groups scattered over several cities and nations. In America, the Antioch Church in Waco, Texas, trains and sends cell group-based planting teams all over the world. All of them have built on a solid theology formed by focusing on Christ in the midst of his body members.

It is obvious to me that while the seeds of the true body of Christ have sprouted here and there, in general the recently developed cell movement may have lost its grasp of this basic truth: Christ is the source and the empowerment of his body parts. Thus, after only a few generations, the term "cell" has become polluted. Must it be redefined in biblical terms to describe the nature of "church?" Do we need a new name or a new definition for "cell?" Do we have a flawed word or a flawed definition and understanding of it? Isn't this the same problem we have with the word "church?"

This is not a new problem. As far back as 90 A.D. Christ spoke to seven churches through John. The problem wasn't in the use of the name "church," it was how they were living out the name. For example, the Ephesians had forsaken their first love.[4] (Imagine, a bride who no longer passionately desires her own husband!)

The *wine* is contaminated, not just the wineskins!

Modern churches focus on large crowds instead of penetrating small segments of society with the light of Christ's presence shining in bodies placed by him in a dark world.

Many churches have adopted new wineskins—new ways of doing church—while still filled with the old wine. The wineskins have been overemphasized. Methods and strategies are not the problem; the *ecclesiology* is defective. It all began as the primitive church left its life as an *organism* to become an *organization*. By the time 1 Corinthians was written (about 67 A.D.), this flaw was already evident as groups gathered without sharing their food with one another.[5] The wine was further contaminated by the formation of the Roman hierarchy and remained in decay through the Reformation period. The nature of Christ's Basic Body in the plan of God for this age has been ignored.

Today, there are churches that are true, authentic expressions of the body of Christ and those that are not. I think it's theologically correct to say that if a group of Christians who assemble don't have certain characteristics as their criteria and foundation, they aren't a real church from a biblical perspective. If the members have Christ in them, they are a part of his body, but their gathering isn't a genuine church. It is important to separate the people who are part of Christ from the church that is something other than what the Bible means by "church," or body of Christ, expressed in a locality.

As you read on, please know that I am *not* saying that traditional church members are not a part of the body of Christ! The difficulty is not with the *people* but rather the theology of the church they embrace using post-biblical traditions composed through the centuries.

The clash with our present patterns of "church" takes place when reference is made to Christ's Basic Bodies, defined once again here for the sake of clarity:

"A community formed and baptized by the Holy Spirit.
Each member is led by the embodied Christ, who edifies and reveals his
presence, power, and purpose through them."

"Are you saying Christ has more than one body?"

Don't think this term is heresy; it is simply a description of how the heavenly church is formed within history. We have no problem understanding there are many parts to church life. We accept divisions of "church" readily to become "Baptist," "Methodist," and so on, and never think of this as heresy, even though it flies in the face of Jesus' prayer that "they all may become one." This thinking fits our paradigm.

The biblical expression of the body of Christ is a small group of believers who are joined by the Holy Spirit to live as members of Christ's Basic Body. Thus, the term "Christ's bodies" must be accepted as the most basic element of the heavenly church.

For example, think of a single skin cell. That cell is not worthless. It is "skin" in its DNA and exists as a basic component. When it is combined with sister cells, it serves to join in covering our bodies. The problem is that few have ever thought of "church" in its most basic form. Be patient with me as I take the definition apart to reveal its full meaning.

"A COMMUNITY"

We must understand the way the term "Body of Christ" is used in Scripture to accurately grasp the concept of *community* (the first word used in the definition of Christ's Basic Body). Ignoring the variations has filtered out important truths. Consider these terms:

A heavenly body

Body is used allegorically in these three passages, referring to the heavenly body of Christ:[6]

Ephesians 1:22, 23: *And God placed all things under his feet and appointed him to be head over everything for the church, which is his body, the fullness of him who fills everything in every way.*

Colossians 1:18: *And he is the head of the body, the church.*

Colossians 1:24: *For the sake of his body, which is the church.*

Can we ever really grasp the enormity of the heavenly church? Our filters restrict our capacity to see this universal body! None but the Holy Spirit can comprehend this giant community encompassing both time and topography.

Individual believers viewed as body

Body is also used to describe the spiritual character of individual believers. We have no problem grasping that each believer is a human body inhabited by Christ:

> Colossians 2:9-12: *For in Christ all the fullness of the Deity lives in bodily form, and you have been given fullness in Christ, who is the head over every power and authority. In him you were also circumcised, in the putting off of the sinful nature, not with a circumcision done by the hands of men but with the circumcision done by Christ, having been buried with him in baptism and raised with him through your faith in the power of God, who raised him from the dead.*

> 1 Corinthians 6:19, 20: *Do you* [singular] *not know that your body* [singular] *is a temple of the Holy Spirit, who is in you* [singular]*, whom you have received from God? You* [singular] *are not your own; you* [singular] *were bought at a price. Therefore honor God with your* [singular] *body.*

A local church body

Throughout the New Testament, *body* is also used to refer to a local body of believers (Note: the following verses all refer to a group, not to an individual, as in 6:19, 20):

> 1 Corinthians 3:16, 17: *Don't you* [plural] *know that you yourselves are God's temple and that God's Spirit lives in you* [plural]*?*

If anyone destroys God's temple, God will destroy him; for God's temple is sacred, and you [plural] are that temple.

1 Corinthians 12:27: *Now you [plural] are the body of Christ, and each one of you is a part of it.*

Ephesians 2:22: *And in him [Christ] you [plural] too are being built together to become a dwelling in which God lives by his Spirit.*

A question people often ask is whether a church composed of Christ's Basic Bodies gathers everyone together. Of course! The entire community gathers together regularly. Gathering the large group is a huge task, but absolutely essential (Acts 20:27 and 1 Corinthians 16:2 document how the early church did so).

On a visit to the *Eglise Protestante Baptiste Oevres et Mission* in Abidjan, Ivory Coast, I asked the pastor, Dion Robert, "How long would it take you to gather all the cell members together for an all-night prayer meeting?" He responded, "When would you like that to happen?" Teasingly, I said, "How about tonight?" He turned to a church leader standing by his side and spoke to him in French. After about ten minutes, the leader returned and said, "We will book a stadium that is free for tonight and the members will gather at 9 P.M." I was shocked when we were taken to a packed soccer stadium that very night!

This cell-based church built their own "temple" for ten thousand, which is used multiple times for worship each weekend. It is a simple structure erected by volunteers from the cell groups. It contains a baptismal pool large enough for thirty or more to be baptized simultaneously. I have personally participated in the baptism of 843 candidates that took several of us hours to complete. The Elim church in El Salvador also has multiple worship services weekly, and annually gathers all its group together in five stadiums to seat nearly 130,000.

A community of body parts

Christ's Basic Body exists for him to fulfill his task of bringing salvation to all nations. Each is to be led by him to disciple all nations. He fills his body members by cells, clusters, and congregations as he proclaims his salvation message through them.

+ *Basic Body*: The cell's "body parts" reveal the presence, power, and purpose of Christ.
+ *Cluster*: Because they share the same core values with sister cells, a specific ministry can take place as they serve together. A cluster is typically from 3 groups up to 12 groups in size.
+ *Congregation*: All cells that are in the same locality will pool their "body parts" to witness to the community.

Christ Leads Ministry through His Basic Body

Examples of this include cells reaching out to their unreached friends through special events (picnics, birthday parties, and other special and not-so-special occasions). The Elim church in El Salvador has two meetings a week: one for edification and one for evangelizing by serving others or meeting together for a meal. A healthy cell is constantly creating events to relate to unchurched persons.

In Singapore, various cell groups (Christ's Basic Bodies) sponsored a "Let's Have a Good Friday" gathering in the homes of the members at Easter time. Special invitations were printed to invite those outside the faith community. Each visitor was given one third of a large nail that had been cut into pieces. Finding the two other pieces, the three persons would look at special *Jerusalem Times* "newspapers" (dated 33 A.D.) posted on the walls of the home. The articles covered the three days between the death and resurrection of Christ. With a questionnaire to complete, they would read all the articles and then answer the questions. The team finishing first with all the right answers was given a gift. The meal's menu had names of items related to the death or resurrection (e.g., "Heavenly Cake"). The meal was followed by a testimony of a believer who had recently come to

Christ. One year, the church also showed a short video clip about people who had experienced a near-death experience. Every year, the new decisions for Christ would equal or exceed the decisions secured in a massive Christmas event at Singapore Stadium (described below).

Christ Leads Ministry through His Cluster

Cluster ministries were used by a church in Macau. The garbage on this island is heaved onto eight-foot-high piles on the corners of streets, often ignored by the city. Members of various Christ's Basic Bodies—identified with T-shirts and headbands—shoveled the garbage into trucks and hauled it away. Amazed apartment dwellers passing by asked them, "Why are you doing this?" Their reply? "Because we serve a Christ who desires to bless your life!"

After cleaning up a block, the members of these groups knocked on the doors of all the apartments in the area, explaining, "We just wanted to thank you for letting us take away your garbage." Although they didn't look or smell like a rose, they were invited in to have tea because the residents were so appreciative!

They used this introduction to secure information for the next step in connection. Along the course of conversation, they asked for the birthdates of the members of the household. The church had a contract with a bakery to provide hundreds of birthday cakes a year. Members of the Christ's Basic Body within that cluster would return each time there was a birthday in the family with a cake to celebrate the occasion! This cluster-based ministry brought hundreds of Macau residents to accept Christ. At the same time, Western missionaries failed to establish a strong church using conventional church planting methods.

Christ Leads Ministry through His Congregation

An example of the congregation of Christ's Basic Bodies sharing a testimony took place each year in Singapore at Faith Community Baptist Church. The twelve thousand seat indoor stadium was booked annually for "Let's Celebrate Christmas." The choirs, dancers, actors, and musicians presented a witness that drew forty-eight thousand Singaporeans, resulting in scores of conversions.

We now touch upon the crux of what the term *Christ's Basic Body* means. First, pause with me. It is my earnest prayer that Paul's prayer in Ephesians 1:17-23 will become true for you as you ponder the depths of this section:

> *I ask—ask the God of our Master, Jesus Christ, the God of glory— to make you intelligent and discerning in knowing him personally, your eyes focused and clear, so that you can see exactly what it is he is calling you to do, grasp the immensity of this glorious way of life he has for Christians, oh, the utter extravagance of his work in us who trust him—endless energy, boundless strength! All this energy issues from Christ: God raised him from death and set him on a throne in deep heaven, in charge of running the universe, everything from galaxies to governments, no name and no power exempt from his rule. And not just for the time being, but forever. He is in charge of it all, has the final word on everything. At the center of all this, Christ rules the church. The church, you see, is not peripheral to the world; the world is peripheral to the church.* The church is Christ's [*Basic*] *Body, in which he speaks and acts, by which he fills everything with his presence.*[7] (Emphasis mine, *The Message*)

Body is used to describe the members selected by the Holy Spirit to form a body inhabited by Christ. The term "community" can be used to describe this intimately bonded group. The body parts inhabited by Christ must be limited in number, typically twelve to fifteen persons to maintain intimacy. It's a matter of communication lines: two people have two communication lines; four people have 12; 10 people have 90; 12 people have 132! When a group exceeds 15, it is rare to find intimacy among more than a handful of the members.

COMMUNITY REQUIRES COMMUNICATION:
Intimacy decreases as the number of body members increases

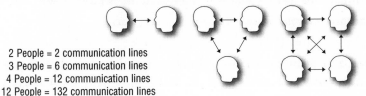

2 People = 2 communication lines
3 People = 6 communication lines
4 People = 12 communication lines
12 People = 132 communication lines

Our personal filters may try to screen out this truth about Christ's "body." We must understand the intimacy required for his basic body to be authentic! The size of the basic body is small. It is the right size to relate to people living in darkness, to reveal the shining of the indwelling Christ. When those basic bodies gather, they can be numbered by the thousands!

Two or three

It is evident that Jesus defined a very small number of people who live in intimacy in his view of "church:"

> Matthew 18:20: *For where two or three come together in my name, there am I with them.* (Note: Christ makes the minimum group number below three, and one person cannot be considered a body or "church" with Christ in the midst.)

Able to judge

Try following this instruction with a "church" of twenty-five to fifty! It doesn't make sense:

> Matthew 18:15-17: *If your brother sins against you, go and show him his fault, just between the two of you. If he listens to you, you have won your brother over. But if he will not listen, take one or two others along, so that 'every matter may be established by the*

testimony of two or three witnesses.' If he refuses to listen to them,
tell it to the church; and if he refuses to listen even to the church,
treat him as you would a pagan or a tax collector.

Both of these can be powerfully performed when the "church" is a body of Christ in which all are able to be close to each other. Body life degrades when more than fifteen people are in a Christ's Basic Body.

I cannot begin to count the number of times pastors I have trained tell me they have "cells" containing from twenty to forty people! Even though much stress was made in their training that no possible intimate communication is possible in a group that large, they failed to grasp this important principle. With fifteen people there are 210 communication lines; with twenty, there are 380! A telephone switchboard would be required for dialogue and any sort of relationship to take place in such a large group.

Able to confess

The confession of sin is also set within the context of a small group:

> James 5:16: *Therefore confess your sins to each other and pray for each other so that you may be healed.* (Note: This references one sick person and a few elders, not the entire gathered community.)

> 1 John 1:9: *If we confess our sins, he is faithful and just and will forgive us our sins and purify us from all unrighteousness.*

While we normally apply the verse above only to an individual confessing sin, the context is obvious: the plural "we" is used, not "I." We are to make *our* confession of our sins to Christ before one another. It is a group activity. How large a group? Small enough to share with "each other." Obviously, this must be a small number, perhaps twelve or less.

While pastoring traditional churches in my earlier years, Christians would come forward during invitation times and say, "Pastor, please pray for me. I want to rededicate my life to Christ." I would ask, "Can you tell me what you have done so I can pray about your situation?" Most of the time they would say, "Oh! It's very personal. Just pray for me." Contrast that with life in Christ's Basic Body: When we share our sins with fellow body members, we all suffer together and are healed together.

Able to edify

Scripture shows the need for a small group to build up one another:

> 1 Corinthians 14:26: *When you come together, everyone has a hymn, or a word of instruction, a revelation, a tongue or an interpretation. All of these must be done for the strengthening of the church.*

The word "everyone" is the Greek *hekastos*. In every single use in Scripture, this word is all-inclusive. "All" means "all," *all* the time! *Hekastos* never refers to an inner group within a larger group. It always refers to the entire group! Question: how large can such a group be if *everyone* is participating? (Obviously, the body in this setting is referring to a very limited number of people.)

Able to bear one another's burdens

The "law of Christ" shows *agape* love. While others may casually pray for others, the participants below are bearing other's burdens, not just observing them:

> Galatians 6:2: *Carry each other's burdens, and in this way you will fulfill the law of Christ.*

Ponder this: how large is *"each other"* here? A group over 15 couldn't possibly know one another well enough to do this!

Able to look after the interests of others

Consider what Christ does to illustrate this in the next verse:

Philippians 2:4: *Each of you should look not only to your own interests, but also to the interests of others.*

His concern for our interests caused him to die on the cross! It is a serious thing to "look not only to our own interests," isn't it?

Able to work out their salvation

We see salvation as a personal transaction between God and man; *Paul* saw it as an activity of the Christ-controlled community:

Philippians 2:12, 13: *Therefore, my dear friends, as you have always obeyed—not only in my presence, but now much more in my absence—continue to work out your salvation with fear and trembling, for it is God who works in you to will and to act according to his good purpose.*

This passage defines securing salvation from the *power* of sin, not from the *penalty* of sin . . . that was the finished work of Christ at Calvary. This ongoing process of being delivered from the power of sin requires accountability within a body. This must be a group small enough to experience such a lifestyle.

Christ binds believers to one another as well as to himself. In 1 Corinthians 12, the first "official act" of the Holy Spirit is to assign each believer a part in Christ's new body:

For we were all baptized by one Spirit into one body—whether Jews or Greeks, slave or free—and we were all given the one Spirit to drink (v. 13).

But in fact God has arranged the parts in the body, every one of them, just as he wanted them to be (v. 18).

Joined and held together

In Colossians 2:19 we are warned not to attempt to live outside Christ-centered community as independent persons who have *"lost connection with the Head, from whom the whole body, supported and held together by its ligaments and sinews, grows as God causes it to grow."*

In the definition of Christ's Basic Bodies, *community* refers to people who are not "joined at the hip" but are rather "joined at the Head." Life in a Christ body is where total transparency exists. There is no need to mask burdens behind a false smile, no expectation that confession will bring condemnation. Confession causes other body members to absorb the pain, the guilt, the shame. No one says, *"I have no need of you!"* (1 Corinthians 12:21-26). Even as the brain responds to a hurt in the body by sending signals and white corpuscles to the site, so fellow body members receive from Christ the Head an empowerment to bring his deliverance to another body member.

I was sharing this truth with a group of Korean pastors in Seoul. One of them interrupted me, saying with a negative sweep of his hand, "You will never find Koreans transparently sharing with each other! That is not a part of our culture as it may be in yours." I replied, "Sir, my culture and your culture are both based on fear and the mistrust of others. I am referring only to life in the kingdom of God! I can assure you that Korean believers *will* experience this freedom to trust and confess burdens and sins when they enter the true community of Christ's kingdom."

This intimacy results in service to God that is quite free in character (Romans 1:9). It also leads to a new freedom toward others, which includes freedom from the fear of other's judgments as well as from one's own attempts to manipulate them.

It is in this Christ-directed community that we find deliverance from secret sins. For example, a serious problem among Christians today is a bondage to online pornography. One man trapped by it joined a Christ's Basic Body and found victory through the meetings. He then gave a password to trusted members that permitted them entry via the Internet to search his computer for signs he had slipped. This community chose to work out their salvation with fear and trembling, knowing God was working within them.

As Christ heals, we witness to observing nonbelievers

The appropriate witness to be provided to nonbelievers requires their *observing* our intimate community life. It is as we transparently confess our struggles and sins that our affirmation of fellow members is revealed. Body members are then observed waiting before Christ to receive his empowering words and actions for healing or ministering. The response he brings through one body member to another one reveals his presence in their midst.

Sounds odd, doesn't it? Yet this is painstakingly described in 1 Corinthians 14:24, 25 (a verse that appears over and over in this book):

> But if some unbelieving outsiders walk in on a service where people are speaking out God's truth, the plain words will bring them up against the truth and probe their hearts. Before you know it, they're going to be on their faces before God, recognizing that God is among you.[8]

"Oikos" is a word that helps us understand Christ's Basic Body

To repeat, *oikos* is a Greek word usually translated as "household." It refers to a house and the people living in it. Thus, it can refer to either the people in the household or to the house itself: "*Day after day, in the temple courts and from house* [oikos] *to house* [oikos], *they never stopped teaching and proclaiming the good news that Jesus is the Christ*" (Acts 5:42).

In 1 Peter 2:5, the term has a special meaning: "*You also, like living*

stones, are being built into a spiritual house [oikos] to be a holy priesthood,
offering spiritual sacrifices acceptable to God through Jesus Christ."

The household [*oikos*] operates along with the Head (Acts 16:15, 34).
Thus the households [*oikos*] became the nucleus for the early life of the
church. (Examples include the house of Priscilla and Aquila at Rome
(Romans 16:3), of Stephanas (1 Corinthians 16:15), of Onesiphorus
(2 Timothy 1:16), and others.) The early body of Christ formed itself
oikos by *oikos*, a far cry from our modern, rampant individualism.

When Jesus sent out the seventy, they were to enter an *oikos* and
meet each person until they found the family member searching for
peace (Luke 10:5-7):

When you enter a house [oikos], *first say, 'Peace to this house*
[oikos].' If a man of peace is there, your peace will rest on him; if
not, it will return to you. Stay in that house [oikos], *eating and*
drinking whatever they give you, for the worker deserves his wages.
Do not move around from house [oikos] *to house* [oikos].

The significance of group conversions reveals that Christ entered
whole families, thus forming his Basic Bodies as the gospel spread. (In
a later chapter we will consider the importance of *oikos* as the focus of
ministry activity, where both *oikonomos* and *oikodomeo* are discussed.)

Into what shapes and purposes and functions can several Christ's
Basic Bodies be formed? When one penetrates a segment of society, the
new believers will come from similar backgrounds. For example, one of
Christ's Basic Bodies in Singapore focused on reaching out to those
who wanted to learn to play an instrument, offering free guitar lessons.
At the end of ten weeks, there were several new believers in this group.
Then, they performed a "concert" for their friends, with all in the group
strumming the instruments together. This led to more friends who
wanted to learn and more guitar groups . . . and more believers!
Two years later, I preached in the congregation whose group sponsored

those guitar lessons. When I entered the meeting room, nearly three hundred believers greeted me . . .and most of them were strumming their guitars during the praise service!

Revisiting *ekklesia*

In the first chapter, I introduced the scriptural use of the Greek word, *Ekklesia*. Here, we must revisit it as it pertains to this discussion of *oikos*. Robert Banks writes, "To embrace the gospel . . . is to enter into community. A person cannot have one without the other. But what *sort* of a community?"[9] The members of this community are described as "called-out ones" or *ekklesia*. Who does the calling out? 1 Corinthians 12:18 explains: "*But in fact God has arranged the parts in the body, every one of them, just as he wanted them to be.*"

A further explanation of how this happens is found in 1 Corinthians 12:13: "*For we were all baptized by one Spirit into one body—whether Jews or Greeks, slave or free—and we were all given the one Spirit to drink.*"

For some, this concept contradicts an old pattern for joining the traditional "church." Assessing what appeals to our personal tastes makes the choice of the particular "church" we join: excellent preaching that does not offend, a style of music we favor, youth and children's programs that our kids enjoy, or the building's location down the street from our home, just to name a few! For some, there may be a *prompting* in the spirit while in a worship service that produces a feeling that "this is the place for me." The baptism by the Spirit into the body is not to a "blob of protoplasm" sitting in rows, staring at someone's bald spot in an auditorium! It is in fact baptism into a Basic Body comprised of members gathered in close proximity with Christ in their midst.

The *ekklesia* we join is not ours to decide . . . it is God's selection. Is it difficult to comprehend and then accept that *ekklesia* should be formed by the Holy Spirit, joining us to those *he* chooses, assigning us the body part he designates, but is nevertheless valid. This is exactly what we see taking place in the New Testament. Ponder the obvious setting of the *ekklesia* described by Paul in Colossians 3: 12-17. This passage obviously requires a limited number in the gathering. Note the intimacy described! These are "selected" people:

> *Therefore, as God's chosen [eklektos, from the ekklesia family] people, holy and dearly loved, clothe yourselves with compassion, kindness, humility, gentleness and patience. Bear with each other and forgive whatever grievances you may have against one another. Forgive as the Lord forgave you. And over all these virtues put on love, which binds them all together in perfect unity. Let the peace of Christ rule in your hearts, since as members of one body you were called to peace. And be thankful. Let the word of Christ dwell in you richly as you teach and admonish one another with all wisdom, and as you sing psalms, hymns and spiritual songs with gratitude in your hearts to God. And whatever you do, whether in word or deed, do it all in the name of the Lord Jesus, giving thanks to God the Father through him.*

Banks summarizes this reality beautifully: "This means that the *ekklesia* is not merely a human association, a gathering of like-minded individuals for a religious purpose, but it is a divinely created affair."[10]

"FORMED AND BAPTIZED BY THE HOLY SPIRIT"

As seen in the previous section, the Holy Spirit is the person of the Godhead designated to join together the body members to become the body inhabited by Christ. Consider the all-important activity of the Holy Spirit in this process:

> John 16:8-11: *He is in the world convicting of sin, righteous-ness, and judgment.*

2 Corinthians 1:21, 22; Ephesians 1:13: *He is the seal given by the Father at the moment we receive Christ into our lives.*

1 Corinthians 12:13: *His further task is to take each member added to Christ and place him where he will function in the life of that body.*

John 14:16, 17: *He becomes the "one called alongside to help" [paraclete].*

John 14:26: *He is the one who teaches us all things Christ commanded.*

Romans 8:26: *He fully participates in the activity of Christ's Basic Body, sharing burdens that cannot be uttered.*

Ephesians 4:7-10 with 1 Corinthians 12:7-11: *He is the agent bringing the gifts of Christ to the body members to be exercised by them.*

In *God's Ultimate Passion,* Frank Viola writes,

The Holy Spirit proceeds from the Father (John 15:26). As such, He is the life of God Himself (Rom. 8:2, 9). More precisely, the Spirit is the bond of love that flows like liquid passion within the communion of the Triune God (Rom. 5:5; 15:30; 2 Cor.13:14). Consequently, the Spirit shares the House, the Family, the Bride, and the Body along with the Father and the Son.[11]

"LED BY THE EMBODIED CHRIST"

The major distinction between a typical small group and a Christ's Basic Body is how it is directed to the place of witness. A man-made group will be led by a human; a Christ's Basic Body will follow his prompting. The members are at his disposal to go where he directs them to reveal his inner presence through their body life. Even as Jesus instructed his twelve apostles to leave their baptizing activities in Jerusalem to follow him to Samaria, so Basic Bodies should receive their ministry mandate from Christ, not church leaders. In Matthew 10:20, Jesus sent out the disciples with these words: *"for it will not be you speaking, but the Spirit of your Father speaking through you."*

Obedience to Christ

This is a new concept for many church leaders as well as members of small groups, yet we see it in operation in the Scriptures. There are numerous examples of people being directed by the Lord to a special destination to declare the kingdom of God and proclaim salvation. We must always remain focused on the direction of Christ's activity in this age: he has already introduced the kingdom and provided the sacrifice of his own life as the door to enter it. His current desire is to draw all who will come to enter his reign over them. He requires a special body to carry his presence to *oikoses* where people need to receive him. Romans 10:14, 15 provides great insight into this truth:

> *But how can people call for help if they don't know whom to trust? And how can they know who to trust if they haven't heard of the One who can be trusted? And how can they hear if nobody tells them? And how is anyone going to tell them, unless someone is sent to do it? That's why Scripture exclaims, A sight to take your breath away! Grand processions of people telling all the good things of God!*[12]

Jesus always directed his disciples to follow him: *"No one can serve two masters. Either he will hate the one and love the other, or he will be devoted to the one and despise the other"* (Matthew 6:24). When we create an institution, we force Christ's Basic Bodies into a position of serving "two masters." Church leaders who exercise "rule" are the marks of the most immature conditions in a local church. It speaks of carnal individuals who have experienced little or no life in the Spirit.

What is the task of the fivefold equippers?

According to Ephesians 4:11-13, He [Christ] *"handed out gifts of apostle, prophet, evangelist, and pastor-teacher to train Christians in skilled servant work, working within Christ's body, the church, until we're all moving rhythmically and easily with each other, efficient and graceful in response to God's Son, fully mature adults, fully developed within and without, fully alive like Christ."*[13] These five gifts of Christ to his body are for the purpose of equipping, not directing. The head of the body is Christ! Those who are mature in the body are to *outfit* the body members, not *control* them. As Christ directs his body to their places of ministry, these five servant ministers are not *over* the members, but *supporting* them, equipping them.

A Christ's Basic Body is composed of a small group who have a special sphere of influence made up of the people they know, their geographical limits, and the skills and talents they possess. If they are challenged by the equipping team to listen and respond to Christ's passionate desire to penetrate their spheres, he will direct them to the people who will experience his presence and power. Each Basic Body will find its target when Christ leads them.

An example of this was seen as the disciples were enjoying baptizing people in Jerusalem.[14] Christ summoned them to go where the Father's heart had been drawing—the much-despised territory of Samaria. If he had not led them there, they would never have chosen to go on their own.

My personal discovery

Many years ago, while pastoring "The People Who Care,"[15] the Lord taught me that the pastoral team's responsibility was to *equip* Christ's Basic Bodies for ministry, not to *create* ministries and look for volunteers. I did not know how this would happen, but I was determined to pound the truth home through my sermons. For many weeks I preached on one theme: "If you *listen*, Christ will guide you to the people group he wants to reach through you!"

Finally, a deacon's wife named Ann came to my office and said, "Pastor, I have been asking Christ who in our area he wants us to reach just as you've challenged. We have dozens of Japanese wives in my neighborhood who feel trapped in their homes. Their husbands leave them alone while they work long hours and travel as executives. These ladies do not speak English, do not understand our culture, our ways of cooking, or our customs. They are totally forgotten and are desperately lonely!"

She went on to show me her research. She wanted to use the Laubach Literacy method to teach English as a second language. She even discovered where the Japanese ladies shopped for their groceries and was given permission to post fliers in the windows of those stores. She concluded her presentation with, "Ralph, the Lord has given me a name for our ministry: HOPE: "Helping Others Practice English."

At the time, we had twenty Basic Bodies that had not yet discovered a vision for outreach. I said, "Ann, when we meet Sunday I want you to address the congregation. Tell them what Christ has shown you and invite any women who wish to transfer into a HOPE group to join you."

She did so, and about eight women came to the front of the room to volunteer. We laid hands on them and set apart the first HOPE group. They were a God-made Basic Body, and Christ-directed! These ladies opened their homes and worked with Japanese women who flocked to participate. Within six months, there were several HOPE Basic Bodies and dozens of Japanese women who met the King and chose to follow him. Husbands and children were added to our fellowship as well.

HOPE went on for several years. So many families came to Christ that we added a young couple to our leadership team to shepherd the Japanese families. Both the husband and wife were missionary kids and grew up in Japan. It was a great fit and the timing was perfect.

This was only the beginning! As the Basic Bodies caught the vision of following Christ's promptings, more than a dozen target groups began—all the result of individuals and groups listening to his voice. Various Basic Bodies came together to target a segment of the community who needed a relationship with Christ through the members' gifts, talents, and passions:

+ Bill and Betty Lottman formed a group called FLOC (For the Love of Children)—to minister to parents of mentally challenged children. This grew into a community of parents attending our worship times and a separate worship service in our children's building for their children! Two godly women formed a group for divorced parents; it mushroomed so fast we had to ask a local Presbyterian church to help us with the large number of those wanting a group.

+ Cal Wheeler formed a group for teens wanting to learn motorcycle repair. They met at his gas station one night a week, and he helped them work on their bikes. Other members of his Basic Body related to the young men and discipled them when they came to Christ.

+ Another group was led by a man who had an air conditioning repair business. They targeted Ph.D. engineers who lived in large homes along Memorial Drive. Believe it or not, they met to explain how these owners could maintain their own air conditioning equipment! By forming friendships, many families came to Christ.

+ Newscaster Cal Thomas formed a breakfast group for key people he met while working as an investigative reporter for a local TV station; on and on his ministry expanded—and in every case, Christ was the guide who led these Basic Bodies to the field he wished to enter.[16]

When I saw this spontaneous Christ-driven ministry, we dedicated one Sunday morning each year for a ministry fair. We created "streets" in our gymnatorium where each team set up a booth and explained their ministries with pictures, samples, and other promotional pieces. Significantly, during this period of time we would frequently add as many as twenty new people to the fellowship.

Contrast this with leadership-directed groups where Christ is not given freedom to lead his body members.

A sad example of man-directed control of groups took place in a church in Singapore, where cell group leaders were given a quota of converts to be baptized every month. One leader who had reached his "quota" for the month said to a convert, "Please don't tell anyone about your experience until after the first of the month. We have already met our quota of new believers for this month. If you wait, I can include you in the cell's quota for next month." While this may seem like an absurd example, it illustrates a defective group under the pressures of a structure, instead of flowing with a divine mandate.

Scripture provides many examples of Christ and the Holy Spirit directly charting the course for ministry activities. Included among them are Philip, guided to the Eunuch: Acts 8:26; Peter, directed to the Centurion: Acts 10:5; Paul, guided through a vision to go to Macedonia: Acts 16:9; the Antioch elders, guided to send forth Paul and Barnabas: Acts 13:1-3.

How does Christ's Basic Body receive his directives?

Looking: Jesus said in John 4:35, *"I tell you, open your eyes and look at the fields! They are ripe for harvest."* First of all, each Christ's Basic Body should carry his life into their *oikos* groups. These are circles of influence, connecting each person to him. A body with twelve members may have as many as ninety-six people in their *oikos* to observe Christ's activity in them.

Next, his new Basic Body may be called to add to that group a special target of people in the community who have no contact with Christians at all. (I have prepared extensive equipping material to explain how members of a Christ's Basic Body can develop target groups.)[17]

Quite often, one or more in the body may have a special talent that becomes a connection point to the target. For example, providing instructions to play a guitar, gourmet cooking, personality development, tennis, basic computer skills, and so forth.

Listening: The members of Christ's Basic Body must learn how to listen to the voice of Christ, not only to be further matured by his power edifying them, but also to receive his burden for searching out unbelievers near their locations. Members will discover how the Holy Spirit "taps them on the shoulder" through daily activities, sensitizing them to people they meet who are responsive to their testimonies. A true Christ's Basic Body will pursue him to feel his burden for a group of unreached persons.

For example, a Houston area high school educates hundreds of undocumented teens from Central America. A leader of a Christ's Basic Body discovered that the fathers of many of the girls were sexually abusing them and their own mothers did nothing to protect them. They needed the financial support of their husbands, and defending their daughters would only serve as the reason the husband used to abandon them in a foreign culture. So, her group sponsored a safe haven for these girls by renting an apartment where they could live with one of the group's singles, a caring woman in her late twenties.

"WHO EDIFIES"

Edification is expressed in Greek by two words that are part of the *oikos* family: *oikonomos* and *oikodomeo*. These two terms reveal the way Christ provides his power to various members of the body to build up other members.

Oikonomos is used multiple times, but we will look at one key passage (Luke 12:42): *"The Lord answered, 'Who then is the faithful and wise manager [oikonomos], whom the master puts in charge of his servants to give them their food allowance at the proper time?'"*

Here we see the Master (Christ) entrusting a household (*oikos*) servant with two things: access to his financial resources and responsibility to spend them at the proper times as the members of the *oikos* have special needs. The flow of resources entrusted to each member of the body is actually the property of the Master. As Christ directs, these resources will be provided to those in the body who have special needs.

Oikodomeo frequently describes the ministry Christ provides by assigning one body member spiritual gifts to build up another member. It contains two words joined together: *oikos* (household) and *domeo* (build up).

A key verse using the term is 1 Corinthians 14:12: *"Even so you, since you are zealous for spiritual gifts, let it be for the edification [oikodomeo] of the church [ekklesia] that you seek to excel."*[18] The precious truth is that Christ, as the head of the body, designates his empowering gifts to fellow body members so they may build up one another.

I have experienced those sacred moments in a Basic Body as one person would share a sin or a burden and the entire group would be silent as they waited for Christ to speak. The Holy Spirit made "groans that words cannot express"[19] on behalf of the member to the group. From Christ's inner presence, the empowering energy (gift) flowed to a body member and ministry would then unfold. At the end, a sense of awe filled the room and the agent of Christ's grace prayed, "Lord! I didn't do that! You used me as your handmaid! Thank you!"

This is the precious lifestyle of Christ's Basic Body. Never forget that when this takes place and the visiting nonbeliever is present, the exclamation will be, "God is certainly among you!" This is the true evangelism of Christ who draws all men unto him by revealing his presence in his body.

"AND REVEALS HIS PRESENCE, POWER, AND PURPOSE"

Are you as exhausted as I with the attempts to counterfeit his presence, power, and purpose by manipulation? I recall a moment in Moscow when in the middle of a "Holy Ghost" Pentecostal prayer meeting, a young college student from Michigan walked over to me and began to blow his bad breath into my face for several seconds. Confused by the experience, I slipped over to one of the knowledgeable charismatic leaders of his team to ask, "Why did that young man blow into my face?" He replied, "He was just doing what Jesus did with the disciples when he breathed on them and said, "Receive ye the Holy Spirit." Later, I learned this is a totally unbiblical fad among some Christian groups.

We live in an age in which we seek to promote the power of Christ in carnal ways. Nonbelievers and immature Christians become cynical because of these excesses and move totally away from any form that expresses supernatural evidence of Christ at work.

We desperately need to see the false as disgusting. The reality appears in splendor in the midst of God's people. The real expression of his presence, power, and purpose *does* appear from time to time! We might quickly fill a hundred pages of reports of the authentic power of God taking place today, but they are the exceptions, not the rule. Authentic healings and deliverances take place and we all rejoice. Yet the end times Jesus spoke about are not yet here. As the traditional hymn declares, "Mercy drops 'round us are falling, but for the showers we plead."[20]

"THROUGH THEM"

Christ's Basic Body can also be referred to as the bride of Christ. The Spirit of Christ, through intimacy with his bride, completes the Father's plan. Through that marriage, he summons all of fallen mankind to "Come!"[21] Through the marriage union of Christ and his bride, many children of God will be birthed.[22]

The children of the union

Christ and his bride will bring forth a family composed of kingdom children. The birth of the first generation would create the next one: *"And let him who hears say, "Come!"* It would further spread to still another generation: *"Whoever is thirsty, let him come."*[23] It would not be limited to any region or generation: *"Whoever wishes, let him take the free gift of the water of life."*[24]

The bride will not be barren. Through her continued intimacy with her husband, she will birth a family to multiply through many generations. Gerald Martin, who serves a large network of cell-based churches,[25] comments:

> An organism is self perpetuating, whereas an organization must be perpetuated externally. An organism left to itself will multiply. An organization left by itself will decline. My grandmother Lehman had 14 brothers and sisters. My mother had 95 first cousins. I have hundreds of second cousins, many of whom I don't even know. There is no Lehman organization that needs to be perpetuated. It just keeps expanding generation after generation. Shouldn't the church be more like that?

We must see the problem and repent!

The tradition-bound "church" is not a holy bride. (We will return to what it *truly* is in a later chapter.) For now, let's concentrate on what God *wants* it to be. It is so hard to see all this from God's viewpoint, for we habitually see things from our own perspective. It is possible for a church to be man-made (not God-made). It will not have a fertile womb. It is barren because it does not experience intimacy with the Bridegroom. Without intimacy there is no childbearing.

I served over four thousand churches for five years in the Evangelism Division of the Baptist Convention of Texas. Less than a hundred of the churches baptized more than a hundred persons a year! A significant percentage of the Baptist churches in Texas had no baptisms at all.

Organizations don't birth children

In today's society, traditional church life may be more of a memory than a reality. George Barna reports that 60 percent of American adults do not attend any church in a typical weekend and twenty million have "dropped out" from church life in the United States alone.[26] Dr. Walter Lumpkin, the late director of the Antioch Institute in Houston, uncovered that 88 percent of the people living in the greater Houston area do not regularly attend a Christian church.[27] The mega churches in my region are swelling with people leaving smaller churches, not from swarms of conversion growth.

The current trend of churchianity is to try to patch the old wineskins. Attention has been focused on how existing structures can be redecorated. New wallpaper pasted over old bricks will supposedly brighten things up and make "church" more attractive to those who have "been there, done that." Becoming more sensitive to the unchurched has caused a trend to offer "new attractions." Church leaders are like the circus owners who seek new acts to draw bigger crowds. Few seem to worry about infertility.

For the most part, the current small group movement is a course correction within the old wineskins of churchianity. They can have many focuses, from cognitive Bible studies, to social work projects and self-help for addictions. Unless each group admits its primary purpose is to receive the indwelling presence of Christ and experience his power, knowing they are fulfilling his purpose, they fall short of a true Christ's Basic Body.

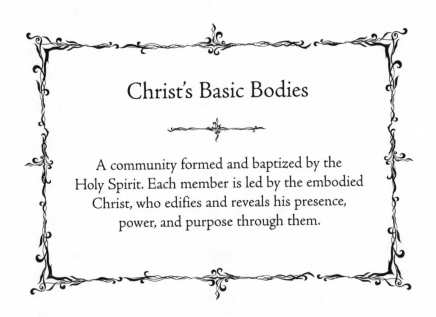

Christ's Basic Bodies

A community formed and baptized by the
Holy Spirit. Each member is led by the embodied
Christ, who edifies and reveals his presence,
power, and purpose through them.

A note from the author:
Much of chapter five is—as explained in the introduction—intentionally
repeated so it will not be forgotten. As you read the familiar concepts, move
through any filters you have discovered to see the depths of what is
being communicated.

The Size and Nature of Christ's Basic Bodies

So if the whole church comes together and everyone speaks in tongues, and some who do not understand or some unbelievers come in, will they not say that you are out of your mind? But if an unbeliever or someone who does not understand comes in while everybody is prophesying, he will be convinced by all that he is a sinner and will be judged by all, and the secrets of his heart will be laid bare. So he will fall down and worship God, exclaiming, "God is really among you!" What then shall we say, brothers? When you come together, everyone has a hymn, or a word of instruction, a revelation, a tongue or an interpretation. All of these must be done for the strengthening of the church. If anyone speaks in a tongue, two—or at the most three— should speak, one at a time, and someone must interpret. If there is no interpreter, the speaker should keep quiet in the church and speak to himself and God.   (1 Corinthians 14:23-28)

Around the world, Christians associate large audiences with church success. Large buildings speak of success. The larger the membership, the greater the proof of accomplishment. *Quantity* is a filter used to determine significance in churchianity. Thomas Bandy writes:

> Large "mega churches" may allow success to outgrow their own avowed spirituality. The growth disciplines of leaders and the spiritual expectations of participants may become weakened, because the organization has more creativity than it can handle. They become preoccupied by the idolatry of members.[1]

Drawing big crowds can be done with little involvement of the power and presence of Christ. It is done with worship bands, choirs, drama, or dance . . . anything and everything is done to attract people to "come to church." However, the true church is composed of those who are "called out" (*ekklesia*). As you will learn, the larger the membership becomes, the less authentic it may become.

In today's churchianity, bigger, "successful" churches hold seminars to show the little ones what they have done to make them get bigger. So successful have they been that many little churches are folding up, giving their properties and memberships to the bigger ones.[2] There are now real estate agents who specialize in selling unused church buildings! Without pews, they make fine boutiques or quaint restaurants, demolished for the value of the land beneath them, or bought and resold for use by other religions.[3]

Here are questions designed to help you overcome the power of any filters you may have about "church."

What is "church?"

When you read the phrase, "the whole church" in 1 Corinthians 14, how does your filter define "church?" Word pictures create images in our minds that become our definitions. Does your word picture allow you to visualize a huge auditorium filled with a thousand people or a small chapel seating 150 as your definition? For many, "church" is a *building*. (For example, "Are you going to church today?").

Other paradigms will say, "What I perceive is not a building, but *people* who have gathered together." Yes! The English word, *church* in Greek *ekklesia*, meaning "called-out ones." One of my favorite German theologians, Adolph Schlatter, grew so disgusted with "church" being the wrong description for *ekklesia* that he used the term "community" as a replacement for "church" in his books.

What comprises the "whole" church?

What size does your filter use to describe "whole": 50 people or more? 100?

The word for "whole" in Greek is *holos* and it simply means, "complete." No specific size is defined. It just means everyone in the *ekklesia* is present. Therefore, the "whole *ekklesia*" in this passage might be as small as two people! Did not Jesus say, *"For where two or three come together in my name, there am I with them"*?[4]

Let's establish that a community of three persons is not a *part* of a church; they *are* the church! It is extremely difficult to change this paradigm, but when we think "church," we must not see a large group of people. The church of God, formed by him at Pentecost, created home groups of believers. In their paradigm, "church" referred to a small group of believers intimately attached to each other with Christ in their midst.

When we examine the location in the temple where the early church went to hear the apostles teach, we see that there was no space for a large assembly. Further, it was the custom in the temple area for a teacher to share with a small group seated around him on the porches. Recall the many activities happening in the courtyards, including moneychangers and sellers of sacrifices. Each apostle probably did not teach more than thirty to fifty at one location (which, by definition, would have been a "large group"). In a very busy and noisy temple court area, and without amplification like we have today, a larger group would have a very difficult time hearing the apostle's voice.

THE "CORPORATE CHURCH" IS FORMED FROM BASIC CELLS, EACH DEFINED AS A "CHRIST'S BASIC BODY."

What term is extraordinary enough to define the true definition of "church" . . . *ekklesia?* A generation ago, we chose the word "cell" for this purpose. It was a pure word apart from an old political use related to communism. Now, *al-Qaeda* has come along and the term "cell" is filled with bad vibes and negative connotations. Another problem with the word: regretfully, the global cell movement now includes "castle builders" instead of "kingdom builders." Today, I do not often refer to "cell groups," although I strongly endorse them in their proper form.

We have already started to understand *Christ's Basic Body* as a term defining basic Christ-directed groups. It defines the true church. The full definition of it will be further explained in this chapter.

What does scripture teach about *ekklesia?*

To limit the harm done by filters, let's begin by finding clues left in Scripture. Put on your Sherlock Holmes hat and let's inspect what God's Word says about life in the *ekklesia* when God formed the body of Christ.

The first clue: Paul's use of the Greek words for "all" (*pas*) and "everyone" (*hekastos*) in 1 Corinthians 14, as related to Christ's Basic Bodies are important clues:

> *Pas:* "all" means "all," in this passage. It is an inclusive adjective that embraces the total, not just a part of the whole. So in the "whole" church, no one is being singled out from the crowd.

> *Hekastos:* This word is very interesting. It is used when the reference is to a plural number, but states that whether a man or woman, *all* are individually included—*no one left out!*

With these words freshly defined and in mind, consider this passage from 1 Corinthians 14:26-29:

> *So if the whole church comes together and everyone [pas] speaks in tongues, and some who do not understand or some unbelievers come in, will they not say that you [plural] are out of your mind? But if an unbeliever or someone who does not understand comes in while*

everybody [pas, plural] is prophesying, he will be convinced by all
[pas, plural] that he is a sinner and will be judged by all [pas,
plural], and the secrets of his heart will be laid bare. So he will fall
down and worship God, exclaiming, "God is really among you!"
[plural] What then shall we say, brothers? When you come
together, everyone [hekastos] has a hymn, or a word of instruction,
a revelation, a tongue or an interpretation. All [pas, plural] of these
must be done for the strengthening of the church. If anyone speaks
in a tongue, two—or at the most three—should speak, one at a
time, and someone must interpret. If there is no interpreter, the
speaker should keep quiet in the church and speak to himself and
God.   (Adapted from *The Message*)

How large can a group of people be to fit the description of what *all*
and *everyone* (no one left out!) are doing? *All* are speaking in tongues.
All are prophesying. *All* are impacting the observers. *All* are participating in causing the unbeliever to fall down and worship God.

This meeting is limited in size by the fact that *everyone* (*hekastos*) is
a participant, not just some of those present. Clearly, this is not a large
gathering. It is intimate enough for total participation. Moreover, there
is no preacher. The group is led by Christ, who manifests his presence
through each member. All are participants, not observers. (The only
exceptions are "unbelievers" and "those who do not understand.")

What conclusion can we draw? Obviously, the group is small
enough that total involvement by all present is taking place. Given some
kind of a time limit for the gathering, perhaps one or two hours, how
many people might actively contribute? It would seem that the size of
the group would be small.

It becomes obvious that "all" and "everyone" must operate within the
limit of fifteen persons. Thus, we may accept that Paul was describing a
small group of people as the "whole" church.

The size of authentic community

In Philippians 2:4, Paul admonishes a gathered Christ's Basic Body: "*Each (hekastos) of you should look not only to your own interests, but also to the interests of others.*" How many people can be involved if that instruction is fulfilled? How many "others" should there be for one person to look after? The awesome thing about this passage is what Paul continues to discuss: the example of Christ's sacrifice on the cross. He says, "*Let this mind be in you . . .*" [5]

This second clue helps us understand that for Paul, the community was small enough for ongoing and intense care for each person in the community. Would you not agree that even fifteen might be too large a number?

He adds more to his admonition about looking to the interests of others: "*Continue to work out your salvation with fear and trembling, for it is God who works in you to will and to act according to his good purpose.*" [6] Note the word "your" used here is plural, not singular. He is describing a community in which "salvation" refers to the *whole*, not just one person. The word "salvation" is not referring to deliverance from the *penalty* of sin nor freedom from the *presence* of sin but rather deliverance from the *power* of sin. He sees this salvation taking place within the Basic Bodies of Christ.

In body life, if one member needs deliverance, the whole body suffers. If you were to experience a cut on your leg, your entire body shares the trauma, right? Therefore, salvation from the power of sin in one person's life impacts everyone.

The size of the meeting places used

Modern day Jerusalem contains a miniature of what the city looked like in the day of Jesus. There is a tourist spot called the "Burnt House" in the old Jewish quarter, an excavation of a residence burned in 70 A.D. It is typical of nearly all the residences of the city. Its largest room only accommodated ten to fifteen people. As the hundreds were dispersed on the night of Pentecost, for the most part they went to small rooms in homes just like this one. The formation of the first house groups defines the *ekklesia* once again as small, not large.

The size and shape of the space available is important for estimating the attendance of both the private and city-wide house churches. Jerome Murphy-O'Connor has collected the archaeological data on a number of first-century villas:[7]

If we removed all the couches from the triclinium, we would end up with space for 20 persons. If we included the atrium, minus any decorative urns, we could expand the group to perhaps 50 persons, provided people did not move around, and some did not mind getting shoved into the shallow pool. The maximum comfortable group such a villa could accommodate would most likely be the range of 30 to 40 persons.[8]

In our generation, gathering a large number of Christ's Basic Bodies together for special events provides powerful witness of how much yeast is within the bread of the society. In El Salvador, the cell groups of the Elim Church rarely numbers more than twelve persons (and when they do, a multiplication of that group will happen quickly). Their combined number of cell members exceeds 130,000 at this writing. In November each year, they lease five football stadiums throughout the city to simultaneously conduct an annual celebration!

That mass of Christians is composed of their home-based Basic Bodies. I sat in one gathering, meeting in a narrow room about ten feet wide and eighteen feet long. Our circle was more of an oval to include the thirteen members present. This is a perfect example of what happens when the focus of ministry changes from building a large weekly gathering to forming Christ's Basic Bodies. The large gathering collects an *audience*; Christ's Basic Bodies meeting in homes form *participants*.

In the pattern God established for the *ekklesia*, the lesser produces the greater. The size of the total number of believers swamps the size of churches that focus solely on attracting crowds.

The "one another" passages

Christ's Basic Bodies, because of his inner presence, enjoy a special relationship. As we have seen, Paul stressed looking after the interests of others. In that spirit, he explained the "one another" verbs. All of these patterns of conduct are built on the "one another" teaching of Jesus in John 13:34, 35: *"A new command I give you: Love one another. As I have loved you, so you must love one another. By this all men will know that you are my disciples, if you love one another."*

As would be expected, the word used for "love" is *agape*, a form of love radically different than brotherly or erotic love. It is the word used for God loving the world found in John 3:16. It is also a form of love that is rooted in the nature and character of Christ. As he indwells his body, the love flowing between them is made possible by him. Here are the "one another" statements:

Romans 12:10	*Be devoted to one another. Honor one another above yourselves.*
Romans 12:16	*Live in harmony with one another.*
Romans 14:13	*Stop passing judgment on one another.*
Romans 15:7	*Accept one another, then, just as Christ accepted you.*
Romans 15:14	*Instruct one another.*
1 Corinthians 1:10	*Agree with one another.*
Galatians 5:13	*Serve one another in love.*
Ephesians 4:2	*Be patient, bearing with one another in love.*
Ephesians 4:32	*Be kind and compassionate to one another, forgiving each other.*
Ephesians 5:19	*Speak to one another with psalms, hymns and spiritual songs.*

Ephesians 5:21   *Submit to one another out of reverence*
                        for Christ.

Colossians 3:13   *Bear with each other and forgive whatever*
                        grievances you may have against one another.

Colossians 3:16   *Teach and admonish one another.*

1 Thessalonians 5:11   *Encourage one another and build*
                        each other up.

Hebrews 3:13   *Encourage one another daily.*

Hebrews 10:24   *Spur one another on toward love and*
                        good deeds.

James 4:11   *Brothers, do not slander one another.*

1 Peter 3:8   *Live in harmony with one another.*

1 Peter 4:9   *Offer hospitality to one another.*

1 Peter 5:5   *Clothe yourselves with humility toward*
                        one another.

1 John 1:7   *Have fellowship with one another.*

All these manners reflect Christ's life in them. It is clear that this lifestyle can only take place in very close relationships. The closeness is further confirmed by another command: "Greet one another with a kiss of love."[9] I shall never forget preaching in St. Petersburg. Russia many years ago. It was the only place where I experienced this command being practiced. For years during communism this group had been underground and persecuted. Such a precious kiss on both cheeks was particularly valuable when it was realized it might be their last time to be together!

It is in the environment of Christ's Basic Bodies that confession and transparency will always be possible because of the "one another" lifestyle. In 1 Corinthians 14:24, 25, we are told all (*pas*) are flowing with the empowerment of Christ's gifts. Edification is taking place. Edification must be preceded by a need for it. Confession *always* precedes edification!

> *But if an unbeliever or someone who does not understand comes*
> *in while everybody is prophesying, he will be convinced by all*
> *that he is a sinner and will be judged by all, and the secrets of*
> *his heart will be laid bare. So he will fall down and worship*
> *God, exclaiming, "God is really among you!"*
>
> (I Corinthians 14:24, 25)

In this Scripture, the unbeliever who falls on his face declaring he
has seen God at work in the group has also had the shock of his life in
hearing the frank confession of sin, of immorality, and of evil deeds. He
enters the group to observe. With shocking transparency, a member of
the body shares a serious, even embarrassing condition. The unbeliever
thinks, "Wow! Can this group be trusted with such a self-revelation?
How will they respond?" The group reacts with tenderness and love.
There is a time of meditation as the body members listen for direction
from Christ within. One by one, the response to the confession is
obviously more than wise words of human origin. Gifts of healing,
discerning, faith, helping the distressed then flow. Because of the "one
another" lifestyle, there is a safe place for each person to be confessional
and to be healed.

This is the authentic evangelism that is so sorely lacking in today's
church life. When unbelievers are exposed to Christ-empowered bodies
the witness born is not a verbal explanation of the "plan of salvation."
The act of salvation, of redemption, of cleansing, is taking place as the
unbeliever watches. He is willing to fall on his face and pour out his
pain and sorrow in front of the group. He says, "Surely God is among
you!" Without the "one another" lifestyle this would never take place.

Use of the plural "you"

Participants in traditional churchianity often read Scriptures
alluding to Christ's Basic Bodies as individual commands because they
do not understand when the word "you" is singular and when it is plural.

For example, the passage we just reviewed in Philippians 2:12-13 confused me for years because I saw it speaking to me as a single Christian: *"Work out your salvation with fear and trembling . . ."* It seemed to be a problem passage contradicting the fact that Jesus had purchased my salvation for me. Besides, Scripture clearly taught that my salvation was *"not by works."*[10]

The first breakthrough came when I realized the three aspects of salvation: freedom from the *penalty* of sin through the cross, freedom from the *presence* of sin by Christ's return, and freedom from the *power* of sin through his life in me. (That was a glorious truth that I wrote about in *The Survival Kit for New Christians*).

But for years I did not recognize another dimension in the passage! Only after I worked through my filters did I see what I had missed! The passage began with an admonition to body members (v. 4) and this passage was also addressed to the *community*, not to individual believers.

For the first time, I realized the "you" in Greek was *plural*, not singular. Paul was referring to a salvation that would be given to the body of Christ: *"work out your [plural] salvation . . . for it is God who is working in you [plural] . . ."* Paul taught that the body parts should have equal concern for each other: *"If one part suffers, every part suffers with it; if one part is honored, every part rejoices with it. Now you are the body of Christ, and each one of you is a part of it."*[11] In an automobile accident, I crushed two vertebrae in my neck. My arms and legs cried out in pain. The healing of my neck finally caused the healing of my entire body.

Suddenly many other plural "you" passages leaped off the pages of my Bible and took on new meaning. Many passages pointed to Christ's Basic Bodies, including 1 Corinthians 11:29: *"For anyone who eats and drinks without recognizing the body of the Lord eats and drinks judgment on himself."* By reading the context, I saw that it is obvious this is linked to Paul's admonitions in verses 17-22. They were having a bad time with body life. The "body of the Lord" to which he refers is not the body of Christ on the cross, but the body sharing the elements of the Lord's Supper! Robert Banks comments on this:

> References to the "body" and "covenant" of Christ (by means of the "bread" and "wine") are not simply two ways of referring to the same thing, viz., and Jesus' death for the sake of others. The term "body" obviously describes the death of Jesus, but the term "covenant" goes on to identify the great benefit that results from that death—a new relationship with God and one another.... Thus the meal they shared together reminded the members of their relationship with Christ and one another and deepened those relationships in the same way that participation in an ordinary meal cements and symbolizes the bond between a family or group. This explains why Paul does not direct his criticisms against the attitudes of people towards the elements of bread and wine ... but against their attitudes and behavior towards one another. [12]

Jesus' reference to handling disputes

Jesus is the source of the first and second references to *ekklesia*. In Matthew 16:18 he states he will be its foundation. In Matthew 18:15-17, he gives instructions about settling a dispute between two brothers. If the two cannot be reconciled to each other, they are to invite one or two others along. If their counsel cannot solve the issue, then the next step is to "tell it to the *ekklesia*:"

> *If your brother sins against you go and show him his fault, just between the two of you. If he listens to you, you have won your brother over. But if he will not listen, take one or two others along, so that 'every matter may be established by the testimony of two or three witnesses.' If he refuses to listen to them, tell it to the church; and if he refuses to listen even to the church, treat him as you would a pagan or a tax collector.*

When Jesus said this, many events would occur before the *ekklesia* would be shaped in the upper room. By his introduction of *ekklesia* to his disciples, he described a community that did not yet exist! This teaching would settle into their hearts and would be taught to others after Pentecost.

Here is a group practicing the "one another" life. A dispute arises. The first step is to see if it can be straightened out between them.

Years ago, I led a Christ's Basic Body that included an accountant and a grocery store manager. Their personalities differed: one used sharpened pencils, the other focused on shelves and cans. During our "get acquainted" stage, they were cordial to each other. Then the group entered the "conflict" stage. The false images of each personality melted away and the authentic persons emerged. One evening, I received a phone call from the accountant: "Ralph, you have just got to talk to Bill. He irritates me! He doesn't have my set of values and you need to get him squared away."

Reminding the accountant of Matthew 18, I indicated that the first step to solve the conflict would require him to be candidly honest with Bill and tell him how he felt. Then, if further negotiation was needed, I would step in with another brother to work through the issue with them. I promised to be in prayer if he would notify me of the time the two would meet. After their confrontation, they worked things out beautifully! Jesus' "step one" worked just fine.

We had another instance, this time in a Christ's Basic Body comprised of divorced parents with children that met in the early 1970s. The covenant they made was that if any two of them wanted to date, they would be shifted to a different group of married couples where they could be mentored and cared for. Because of that agreement, the men and women treated each other like brothers and sisters. Then a newly divorced woman was invited to attend the group. From the first meeting, she had her eye out for one of the men!

Dawn was the leader of the group at the time. She called me and said, "Ralph, this gal is barely out of her marriage and is trying to seduce one of the guys and he is oblivious! He can't see what is happening. I want you to talk to this girl for us."

My reply? "Sorry, Dawn. That's not God's way. You talk to her as the leader of your group. Let me know what happens." A few days later she phoned: "She told me to mind my own business! She is not yet a believer and I do not want to drive her away. What should I do?"

I read her the passage from Matthew 18 and suggested she call a closed meeting of the group (after all, it was Christ's Basic Body) and confront her with the entire group present.

The meeting started with the guys being surprised that they had not caught on to what the lady was doing; the women in the group took charge and spoke lovingly to her about the way she was going about finding another husband when her divorce had not yet been processed.

She ran into the bathroom screaming, "I'm going to kill myself!" As she locked the door, those on the outside heard her break a glass cup on the floor.

Dawn woke me up about 11:00 P.M. to say, "Ralph, she's in the bathroom and is going to commit suicide. Come right now!"

"No," I said, "No one commits suicide with a whole roomful of people around. Call her bluff. Shout through the door, 'Please climb into the tub before you cut your wrists so I won't have to clean the blood off the rug!' She'll come out soon enough." (Of course, I'd never recommend doing this today, but it seemed right at the time!)

Sulking, she came out of the bathroom and sat down when she realized her manipulative threats had no power. The group then ministered to her and I, too, got involved in some heavy-duty counseling in the days that followed.

I have dozens of stories like this. The principle of Jesus works—but *only in Christ's Basic Bodies* where "one another" life is being practiced.

The "assembling together" in Hebrews

To really understand the absurdity of what personal filters can do to Scripture, consider this statement in Hebrews 10:25, taken out of context: *"Let us not give up meeting together, as some are in the habit of doing."* This is a favorite stick to swing from the pulpit toward delinquent church attendees who only show up on Easter Sunday. It is not talking about Sunday worship services at 11 A.M. at all! Let's look at the context:

> And let us consider how we may spur one another on toward love and good deeds. Let us not give up meeting together, as some are in the habit of doing, but let us encourage one another—and all the more as you see the Day approaching.[13]

Was the writer talking about traditional church services where people silently sit in rows and listen to a sermon? Not at all! This is speaking of a meeting of Christ's Basic Body. In this context, the people are exhorted both before and after the key statement to practice the "one another" lifestyle. When you take a text from the context, you get . . . nonsense!

Conclusions

We cannot think first of a universal body of Christ as "the church." He does not first dwell in a universe, He dwells in bodies. We must rethink all our concepts of "church." It does not start with a congregation or a building. It starts with called-out men and women who are brought into intimate community by the Holy Spirit. All Christ's bodies stand alone as the *ekklesia*.

At the same time we confirm the true church is composed of a small body, we reject that any single Christ's Basic Body is independent. All become one worldwide *ekklesia* and together make it possible for Christ to fulfill his mission in this age of history.

A study of Scripture limits the size of Christ's Basic Bodies from twelve to fifteen persons. Never, ever refer to this as a generic, all-purpose "small group." It is the sacred creation of God, inhabited by his Son. We cannot settle for any term or description that assembles small groups who exist apart from the clear ownership of Christ directing them.

We have viewed the church upside down!

If we are to establish authentic *ekklesia,* we need to let the church's large gatherings flow naturally from the establishment of Christ's Basic Bodies. This obviously creates a huge problem for churchianity in its present form, but that is not a reason to ignore what we have done to the sacred bride of Christ and not make things right.

The authentic New Testament church will emerge in the future. *It must!* Some who read these pages will have too much invested in the present structures to do anything about traditional church life. They are agents of God for this time. They are deeply loved by him, but must realize how the Holy Spirit is grieved to see millions of church members who may never experience the ministry they were set apart to perform.

Christ's Basic Bodies must not be controlled by man. Instead, they desperately need apostles, prophets, evangelists, pastors, and teachers who will equip all (*pas*) to be body members. The Lord of the harvest can be trusted to thrust his presence in his bodies into whitened fields.

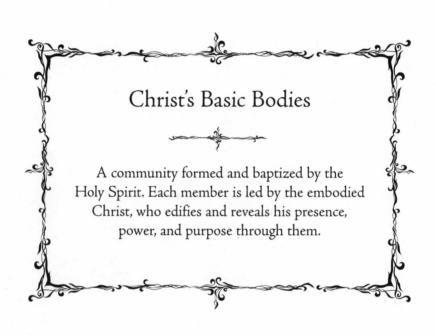

Christ's Basic Bodies

A community formed and baptized by the
Holy Spirit. Each member is led by the embodied
Christ, who edifies and reveals his presence,
power, and purpose through them.

chapter six

Temple Furniture

Jesus left the temple and was walking away when his disciples came up to him to call his attention to its buildings. "Do you see all these things?" he asked. "I tell you the truth, not one stone here will be left on another; every one will be thrown down."

(Matthew 24:1, 2)

How would you define the word "furniture?" *Webster's Dictionary* defines it as "equipment that is necessary, useful, or desirable." We view furniture through our personal filters, revealing much about our value systems. Whether personal or community furniture, our furniture reveals our personal values:

Personal furniture

What furniture is supporting you as you read this? A chair? A bed? A couch? These are necessary furnishings that support our bodies. Their usefulness is temporary but necessary. A bed is sought out when it's time to sleep. A couch in a formal living room may be used for only a few hours a year or it may be used only when people come to visit. However, an easy chair in the den may be used for many hours each week.

Community furniture

"Community furniture" supports us as we live in society. Consider the branch of the bank you use. You need it to make deposits and payments, but you don't spend time there when you're not withdrawing money or making a payment to an account. Then there's the hospital, which is always there if you need it, but you never use it unless you absolutely must!

Government furniture

There is also "government furniture." We dutifully pay taxes because it funds roads, armies, police protection, and firemen. Don't forget the "school furniture." We have a long-term relationship with the classroom, but it's certainly a relief when we don't need them and can hang a diploma on the wall that says, "Been there, done that!" We then support the institution as alumni so others will profit from it.

Let's add one more structure to our inventory of community furniture: the "religious meeting place." It is a desirable accessory to a small segment of the total population, visited approximately once or twice a week. Like other community furniture, it has significance only when it is used. The rest of the time it sits empty, displaying its steeple to the passersby saying, "Hey! Notice me!"

People use the wrong noun to refer to this religious meeting place. They refer to it as "church." A hospital is called a "hospital." A school is called a "school." But a "religious meeting place" is improperly called a "church." (As we learned earlier, the word *church* as used in the Bible comes from the Greek *ekklesia*, which translates into the English as "called-out people," not a building.)

Consider the constant misuse of the word: "Are you going to *church* today?" Or, "We go to *church* every Sunday." This usage refers to a building, not to people. Someone says, "I go to Mill Road *Church*." The immediate mental image in the minds of the listener and the hearer is a building on Mill Road. Can you imagine how impossible a task it would be to persuade Christians worldwide to revise their definition of religious buildings and call them "assembly halls," "meeting places," or something else?

Ugh! So ingrained is this contemptible misuse of the word *church* that it is almost impossible for us to use it in a biblical sense. That's why the Christian community to which I belong in Houston refers to itself as "The Touch *Family*." We have determined to refer to ourselves as the *called-out people, a Christian community,* not a "church."

In this book, I have worked hard to use the word "church" when it defines the mental image it brings forth: a building with pews, preachers, and programs. I wonder why we don't call these religious buildings what they really are—fishbowls! While it is certainly not true of every churchgoer, these structures include many who enter them to swim out of habit or custom.

THE DESIGN OF "CHURCH" BUILDINGS DESTROYS COMMUNITY

In the *Celletter* of St. Boniface Catholic Church (Pembroke Pines, Florida), Father Al Lauer writes,

> For the first three hundred years of Christianity, the Church met in homes (see Romans 16:5). Then, after the Roman Emperor Constantine stopped the persecution of the Church, he built the first church building in the Western world on land owned by the Laterini family. This church was eventually dedicated to St. John the Baptist and was called the Basilica of St. John Lateran. This parish church was built to help the home churches be more deeply united with each other and the Universal Church. Thus, the parish church was originally intended to serve the home churches.[1]

This first attempt at constructing a gathering place for home groups was the primary step toward the formation of formal buildings erected by Catholic leaders. It was originally recognized as a "meeting place" where home groups could assemble for joint fellowship. The formation of rooms with rows and rows of pews had not yet developed. Fostering fellowship between the home groups was the original intention.

A further development took place that changed everything. After the church was born, it was slowly split into "clergy" and "laity."

No longer would the people of God be commissioned to perform the tasks of the community. *"All authority on heaven and earth"* was now placed in the hands of "hired holy men."

Those edicts became the reason for religious buildings being so constructed that the laity would forever sit in rows and view the faces of the clergy, elevated above them by a platform. The clergy took control of religion and took the title "priest." Ministry no longer belonged to common Christians seated in the pews. Michael L. Papesh writes,

> The priesthood of the ordained becomes an active priesthood of status and office connected to the Eucharist, not a priesthood of service connected with a particular community of faith. . . . The care of souls is reduced to providing sacraments with canonical correctness. The common priesthood of the laity, now understood as a passive priesthood, depends on ordained priests. Ministry becomes, by definition, something done solely done by the ordained.[2]

Whether built using clapboard or gold-leafed panels, these buildings, constructed for centuries, have all guaranteed that "holy men" have elevated stages to strut and speak to the humble audience. Thus, church became theater, complete with a stage for the actors and the candles. Audience participation might include bowing, chanting, and singing, but there would never be *community life* in those services.

Millions of people, both Catholic and Protestant, now define church as an auditorium (sanctuary) where they sit while being instructed on how to "act" by the expert behind the pulpit. The intimacy of community described in the New Testament is lost. No longer do hands, feet, and inward parts need each other. There is no possibility of *"looking to the interests of others"* (Philippians 2:4) when all we see are the backs of heads in the rows in front of us. Sadly, Christians in the pews are sometimes invited to "turn around and greet the person sitting behind you." What a sick attempt at fostering community!

I was impressed when I saw this photo of fish tied together in rows, dead and dried, taken at a market in South Korea. All the fish have their mouths open as though they were ready to be fed, but in reality no digestion is possible.

The picture reminds me of a childhood poem used by folding fingers and saying,

Here's the church,
And here's the steeple.
Open the doors
And see all the people... *sitting in rows!*

Satan knew that because of one vote made by a few men at the Council of Chalcedon in 451 A.D., he could forever destroy the most precious ingredient of God's kingdom—*life lived in community*. Bill Beckham in *The Second Reformation* writes:

> The Creator once created a church with two wings: one wing was for large group celebration, the other wing for small group community. Using both wings, the church could soar high into the heavens, entering into His presence and do His will over all the earth.
>
> After a few hundred years of flying across the earth, the Two-Winged Church began to question the need for the small group wing. The jealous, wicked serpent, who had no wings, loudly applauded this idea. Over the years, the small group wing became weaker and weaker from lack of exercise until it virtually had no strength at all. The Two-Winged church that had soared high in the heavens was now for all practical purposes one-winged.
>
> The Creator of the church was very sad. He knew the Two-Winged design had allowed the church to soar into His presence and do His bidding. Now with only one wing, just lifting off of the ground required tremendous energy and effort. And if the church did manage to become airborne, it was prone to fly in circles, lose its sense of direction, and not fly very far from its takeoff point. Spending more and more time in the safety and comfort of its habitat, it grew contented with an earth bound existence.
>
> From time to time, the church dreamed of flying into the presence of the Creator, and doing His work all over the earth. But now, the strong large group wing controlled every movement of the church and doomed it to an earth-bound existence.
>
> In compassion, the Creator finally stretched forth His hand

and reshaped His church so it could use both wings. Once again the Creator possessed a church that could fly into His presence and soar high over all the earth, fulfilling His purposes and plans.[3]

I find absolutely nothing wrong with lecture seating provided for teaching and worship. The psalmist wrote, *"I will give you thanks in the great assembly; among throngs of people I will praise you"* (Psalm 35:18). There is a time and place for auditoriums. *But we cannot destroy the other wing of the church.*

LEARNING FROM COUNT VON ZINZENDORF

The furniture that supports the true body of Christ is constructed for the kingdom of God using spiritual supplies. After the Reformation that began in 1517, the first generation was filled with fire and zeal, as evidenced by Luther's *A Mighty Fortress Is Our God.* But the clergy-laity cleavage remained intact. Lutheran buildings continued to create rooms where the clergy presided over the laity.

Community life did not accompany Luther's awareness that Christ's death on the cross atoned for our sin. It would take a different movement of the Reformation for community to be rediscovered. We pay tribute to Count Von Zinzendorf, the man God used to develop it. The Comenius Foundation shares about the life of the man who is responsible for this return to New Testament life:

Nicholas Ludwig, Count Zinzendorf, was born in Dresden in 1700. He was very much a part of the Pietist movement in Germany, which emphasized personal piety and an emotional component to the religious life. This was in contrast to the state Lutheran Church of the day, which had grown to symbolize a largely intellectual faith centered on belief in specific doctrines.

He believed in "heart religion," a personal salvation built on the individual's spiritual relationship with Christ. . . . In 1722, he was approached by a group of Moravians to request permission to live on his lands. He granted their request, and a small band crossed the border from Moravia to settle in a town they called Herrnhut, or "the Lord's Watch." Zinzendorf was intrigued by the story of the Moravians, and began to read about the early Unity at the library in Dresden. His tenants went through a period of serious division, and it was then in 1727 that Zinzendorf left public life to spend all his time at his Berthelsdorf estate working with the troubled Moravians. Largely due to his leadership in daily Bible studies, the group came to formulate a unique document, known as the "Brotherly Agreement," which set forth basic tenets of Christian behavior. . . . There followed an intense and powerful experience of renewal, often described as the "Moravian Pentecost." During a communion service at Berthelsdorf, the entire congregation felt a powerful presence of the Holy Spirit, and felt their previous differences swept away. This experience began the Moravian renewal, and led to the beginning of the Protestant World Mission movement.[4]

What did Zinzendorf construct? The furniture of fellowship! He dedicated his property for the use of the community of God's people. Herrnhut became God's furniture!

Kingdom furniture

If Bill Beckham's two winged-church is to fly, it obviously needs a gathering place for the Great Congregation.[5] I find nothing immoral about space reserved for the worship of God and for general instruction. But what kind of furniture fits the Christian community when Christ's Basic Bodies gather?

There is an important reason why the communities should move "from house to house" as mentioned in Acts 5:42. There's a crucial spiritual issue involved here. In 1 Corinthians 14:24, 25, we see Christ empowering body members so friends and relatives will say, *"God is among you!"* That takes place in Christ's Basic Bodies, not in large auditoriums.

But when we build new structures, why cannot these first units be gymnatoriums rather than auditoriums? In 1972 we built the "Touch Center" in Houston, offering a single room used for celebrations, basketball, roller skating, banquets, parties, lock-ins for teens, and many other activities. Six hundred chairs could be stored in a matter of thirty minutes after we used it as an auditorium. Everyone folded up his chair, put it on a rolling cart, and the carts were wheeled into large closets built into the side of the room. This multiple-use space worked beautifully and saved us hundreds of thousands of dollars that would have been invested in separate facilities.

We are at a time in church history when we need to see new structures that foster community living as well as large gatherings for worship and teaching. Meeting places can become places for prayer, training, small group interaction, and witness.

Kingdom furniture for the community

I have been brainstorming a concept for using property to reach the unreached. As I reflect on the millions of Houstonians who would not be caught dead in a church building, I am excited about another possibility. Please know that as I write, this is only a dream, but I can see it as very effective in mingling the people of God with the unreached population.

Consider a large store (grocery or general merchandise) that has gone out of business. One of the advantages of securing such a large space is that it will be located where people shop. Parking will already be available. Consider the open-room concept used by grocers. By dividing the huge space into categories, people now shop for vegetables, meat, canned goods, snacks, books, and other items. People feel free when entering space so designed.

Now think about that same store converted into a meeting place with twenty thousand square feet and a fourteen-foot ceiling. By creating cluster areas, a "market place" could be designed for use by both believers and unbelievers. There could be clusters of lounge chairs for small groups, a snack bar, a fenced play area for children, a computer center, and may other areas. This could be a connecting place between Christ's Basic Bodies and the surrounding community, meeting needs of families and singles of all ages. It could be kept open all week.

Whether this proposal is an answer or not, we need to rethink the way "church" is seen as "community property" that is used only by Christians for a few hours a week. A part of the evolution of the church will involve transitioning millions of square feet of buildings now misused or unused for more appropriate activities that will provide for kingdom ministries.

The direct mission of Christ as he expressed it in Luke 4:18, 19 sent him to the poor, the brokenhearted, the captives, the blind, and the bruised. Real estate now in the possession of God's people can be revamped to contribute to this task.

For example, in Conroe, Texas, a fellowship of thirteen churches has converted unused Sunday school rooms into spaces for homeless families, called the Interfaith Hospitality Network (IHN). The congregations provide food and spare clothing. Each family may stay one week at each location and may move from church to church until they stabilize and find a permanent place to live. They are also assisted in finding employment. In a typical IHN, half of the guests are children, most of whom are under six years of age.

This nationwide movement began when Karen Olson regularly encountered homeless people on her way to New York City from her New Jersey residence. As a result of her vision, the Family Promise movement has established 114 affiliates in 37 states, using the services of more than 100,000 volunteers and 4,000 congregations, supporting more than 17,000 homeless family members annually.[6]

In Waco, Texas, Mission Waco sponsors a church for the homeless that meets under Interstate 35.[7] This ministry has converted the former Central Presbyterian Church property to create an easily accessible social service center for the poor and marginalized. Mission Waco is supported by a collaboration of organizations which assist the people's needs. Much of the downstairs area of the main building was renovated to provide intake, case management, emergency shelter, voucher distribution, showers, laundry, haircuts, and meals.[8]

For centuries, church buildings have been reserved for a few hours of occupancy per week. It is a scandal that must be faced! These structures are certainly a part of the wood, hay, and stubble that will be burned with holy fire at the Bema judgment.

"Somewhere to be"

In *A Place For You*, Paul Tournier describes the importance of a tree having deep roots in order to exist.[9] Every person looks for a community attachment. That is why Christ's Basic Bodies are God's answer for those seeking "somewhere to be." This is an environment in which people care about each other, where total transparency is possible, and where healing of hurts is the priority. The physical erection of a building alone will never provide a place for community, found only in close relationships.

Tournier goes on to discuss the importance of people through the centuries desiring to establish a physical place for their deities, a way of localizing where the invisible can be contacted.[x] God created such a place for Israel: the golden ark, a box that contained the testimony of the covenant. It was portable and carried in their midst as they traveled. In the portable tabernacle, above the ark hovered a cloud of smoke by day and a pillar of fire by night.

Israel was structured into groups of ten as their "place to be." God's presence was provided in an ark containing the covenant. Later, Solomon built an ornate temple and dedicated it with these words: "*But will God really dwell on earth with men? The heavens, even the highest heavens, cannot contain you. How much less this temple I have built!*" (2 Chronicles 6:18). But this localization of God had many dangers related to it. His presence was restricted in the minds of the people to a place. He was not present everywhere. He was only in one spot.

This danger continues today. Many will excuse the profuse investments to erect buildings with stained glass windows and gold domes boasting, "We do this to show the unbelieving world that we greatly honor our God." In fact, those who do not ever enter the structure cynically ask, "Who is really honored by this opulence? Does it minister to the poor, the blind, and the broken-hearted? Who are these people trying to fool?" Church buildings often reveal more of the members' own pride and values for luxury than their desire to honor and worship God!

Thus, when redemption was secured for all men at Calvary and Christ began his assignment to declare this news to all men, he entered a very special ark of the covenant. It would be mobile, able to enter any hovel or community in the world, at any point in history. He chose a very special temple in which to dwell, explained by him in John 2:21 as his body.

> *Don't you know that you yourselves are God's temple and that God's Spirit lives in you? If anyone destroys God's temple, God will destroy him; for God's temple is sacred, and you are that temple.*[11]

> *For we are the temple of the living God. As God has said: "I will live with them and walk among them, and I will be their God, and they will be my people."*[12]

*In him the whole building is joined together and rises to become a
holy temple in the Lord. And in him you too are being built together
to become a dwelling in which God lives by his Spirit.*[13]

It is a solemn thing to be a temple of the living God! Each Christ's
Basic Body is that sacred temple.

All world religions place God in a structure. From the scores of
carved images on a Hindu temple to the opulent sanctuaries of
America, the deceptions are the same. In these last days, men will be
forced to decide what to do with all the church structures left standing,
looking like gravestones identifying the dead structures they contained:
*Here lies the First United Church of the City. Monument preserved by the
Historical Society.*

Theological Issues

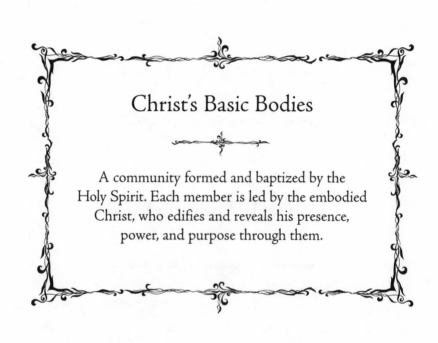

Christs Basic Bodies

A community formed and baptized by the Holy Spirit. Each member is led by the embodied Christ, who edifies and reveals his presence, power, and purpose through them.

The Community of the Godhead

And if anyone does not have the Spirit of Christ, he does not belong to Christ. But if Christ is in you, your body is dead because of sin, yet your spirit is alive because of righteousness. And if the Spirit of him who raised Jesus from the dead is living in you, He who raised Christ from the dead will also give life to your mortal bodies through his Spirit, who lives in you.

(Romans 8:9-11)

Much confusion exists in our generation about the significance of the Son and the Spirit in the activity of God. Paul made it clear in Colossians 1:19 that Christ is central in the revelation of God and when he is present the Father and the Spirit are present as well.

We understand the nature of God only through the filters of our own fallen nature, which is the opposite of God's nature.[1] We are self-seeking and think first of ourselves. Thus, our view of God is distorted by our self-centered personalities. This is first demonstrated by Eve's choice, even in her pre-fallen state. She chose to disobey God when Satan promised that by doing so she would become like God.

UNDERSTANDING THE GODHEAD

God is not like us. He is a community of three persons: the Father, the Son, and the Holy Spirit.[2] He does not function at any time as three individuals. Instead, each of these three persons has a distinct personality, but they never operate separately. The Father is God. The Son is God. The Spirit is God. They cannot be studied individually, since they are not individuals. (That is what the illustration is

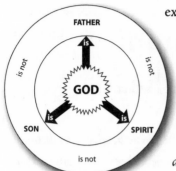

explaining with the words "is" and "is not" between the Father, Son, and Spirit.)

The doctrine of the Trinity is encapsulated in Matthew 28:19, where Jesus instructs the apostles: *"Therefore go and make disciples of all nations, baptizing them in the name of the Father and of the Son and of the Holy Spirit."*[3] He indicates thereby that the Holy Spirit is a person, too, just as are the Father and the Son. Paul, in authorizing certain instructions to the early community, wrote, *"It seemed good to the Holy Spirit and to us not to burden you with anything beyond the following requirements"* (Acts 15:28). He very clearly considers the Holy Spirit a person capable of expressing the same thoughts and ideas he and the apostles shared.

God the Father is defined by his relationship to the Son.[4] He is only "Father" in relation to the Son, not the Spirit. The Spirit is "breathed out," not born. Thus, the Spirit cannot be seen as a second son of the Father. He proceeds directly from the Father.[5] He does not proceed equally from the Son. If this were so, the Son would be the second Father and there would be two different origins for the divine Spirit.[6] The Holy Spirit empowers us to pray like Jesus and manifest spiritual gifts. Through the Holy Spirit we are filled not with him alone, but also with the Father and the Son.

In Colossians, Paul instructs us not to accept the *"basic principles of the world."* He points out that in Christ *"dwells all the fullness of the Godhead bodily."*[7] Incarnated by the Son, Jesus was able to say, *"Anyone who has seen me has seen the Father."*[8]

Christ refers to all three identities in one sentence when he says, *"But the Helper, the Holy Spirit, [1] whom the Father [2] will send in My name, [3] He will teach you all things, and bring to your remembrance all things that I said to you."*[9] As the Son came in the Father's name, so the

Father was to send the Spirit in the Son's name, with divine authority and power to do two great things: first, to teach them all things and second, to bring to remembrance all things Christ had said to them.[10]

The Spirit helps us to communicate with God. Romans 8:15, 16 explains when we cry, "Abba, Father," it is the Spirit bearing witness with our spirit that we are children of God. *"In the same way, the Spirit helps us in our weakness. We do not know what we ought to pray for, but the Spirit himself intercedes for us with groans that words cannot express. And he who searches our hearts knows the mind of the Spirit, because the Spirit intercedes for the saints in accordance with God's will."*[11]

As the Godhead chooses to reveal the invisible presence at the highest level, we see that the ambassador who is sent is the Son: *"Whoever receives Me, receives not Me but Him who sent Me."*[12] But the Son contains all the Father is: *"I and the Father are one."*[13] The Spirit fully participates in all that takes place between the Father and the Son and was present at the baptism of Jesus.[14]

Dr. Ron Rhodes writes, "This goal of exalting Jesus may account for why the Holy Spirit is not mentioned as prominently in Scripture as Jesus (and even the Father). The Holy Spirit, who inspired Scripture, humbly points away from Himself and exalts Jesus in the pages of Scripture."[15]

A study of Romans 8:9-11 reveals the way Paul saw the Godhead intertwined as he manifests his presence in us. The entire Trinity is intertwined in these references:

> *But you are not in the flesh but* in the Spirit, *if indeed* the Spirit of God *dwells in you. Now if anyone does not have* the Spirit of Christ, *he is not His. And if* Christ is in you, *the body is dead because of sin, but the Spirit is life because of righteousness. But if* the Spirit of Him who raised Jesus from the dead *dwells in you,* He who raised Christ from the dead *will also give life to your mortal bodies through* His Spirit *who dwells in you* (NKJV, emphasis mine).

How does the Godhead react to sin?

Each member of the Trinity has different roles. This causes them to approach "sin," the criminal theft of the self-ownership of our own life, in different ways:

God the Father is holy. He cannot look upon sin.[16]

Jesus is no less holy when he became sin for us.[17]

The Holy Spirit is no less holy because he indwells the sinner.[18]

Their different roles (thankfully) guarantee that we can have access to the unseen God by the power of his Spirit.

Paul's view of Christ and the Spirit

When writing Ephesians, Paul is very careful to focus on the "great secret" hidden through the ages: Christ is the Head of the *ekklesia* and supplies all his body needs by indwelling it. He resides along with the Holy Spirit and the Father in his basic body and is the source of all the gifts. He is also the one who gives to his body the fivefold equippers for strengthening of its ministry.

I was quite surprised to hear a believer argue passionately that "only the Holy Spirit is among us today. Christ's work was completed when he ascended to heaven after the rapture." This flies in the face of all Paul taught and demeans the presence and power and purpose of Christ in our generation. Adolf Schlatter wrote,

Christ's unity with God does not result in Paul's positioning a division . . . in which he assigned one part of his thinking and willing to the Christ and another to the Spirit. By virtue of his unity with God, Christ has access to man's inner life, and man owes him all internal processes that prove to be true and good.

What Paul does in the Spirit is not placed beside what he does in the Christ as a separate area. The Christ is God's; the Spirit is God's as well: thus there is unity between the effects of Christ and those of the Spirit. . . . The community belongs to the Christ entirely and forever, and beyond him nothing exists for it. . . .The work of Christ for the community has as its prerequisite the work of the Spirit, because the Spirit brings about the confession by which the community witnesses to Christ's lordship. . . He unites believers to a community and equips it with the powers by which it performs its service as the body of Christ (1 Cor. 12:3; 2 Cor. 4:13; Rom. 15:30; 1 Cor. 12:13; Eph. 4:3 Phil. 2:1).[19]

The mission of the Godhead

The very nature of God is shown by the activity of the Trinity. There is a mission to be performed. That mission is to reclaim mankind from self-ownership, for God to possess each human in such a way that he will express his own divine Spirit through human spirits. God the Father chose to send the Son, and together they commissioned the participation of the Spirit.

The first two assignments of Christ required him to be incarnated in the body of Jesus. In Jesus, he revealed the kingdom of God had come to the earth with supernatural powers. Also in Jesus, he became the Lamb that would atone for the sin of all mankind. (More on this in chapter eight.)

He had a third mission to complete. It would require him to reveal God's kingdom and redemption to all humanity through all centuries of time. That assignment required a special body. The Spirit would prepare it so the Son could redeem many from all cultures. Drawing unbelievers is the activity of God, not man. Christ is the Lord of the harvest. He occupies his new body to manifest his presence and power to harvest the whitened fields.[20]

Christ, the Anointed One

The word "Christ" in Greek is *kristos*, translated "anointed." It describes being *set apart*, consecrated to fulfill a special task. It is used as an adjective as well as a noun. In passage after passage it refers to the activity of the Son within the community of the Godhead. In Acts 10:38 we are told, "*God anointed Jesus of Nazareth with the Holy Spirit and power.*" The reference to the Holy Spirit here is in the context of Christ the Son entering Jesus as Mary conceived him, the man who was to be incarnated by the Anointed (empowered) One.

In Acts, "Christ" is also used as a title: "*This is how God fulfilled what he had foretold through all the prophets, saying that his Christ would suffer.*"[21] It is important to understand that when the invisible God chose to reveal himself, his assigned agent would be the Son—the Christ, the Anointed One—who would fulfill all assignments representing the Godhead. "*He has been installed in the royal office by the will of God and possesses lordship by the commission of God.*"[22]

The Father, the Son, and the "sons"

Jesus continually explains the intimate relationship of Christ to the Father. A beautiful thought is expressed by joining two verses that refer to the birth of Christ. Acts 13:33 refers to the prophecy in Psalm 2:7. The Father says, "*You are My Son; Today I have begotten you*" (NKJV).

In response, Hebrews describes the cry of a tiny baby who has just arrived from the womb of Mary—a baby's wail to humans—but in heaven, the Father heard, "*I have come to do your will, O God.*"[23] Therefore, when Christ came into the world, he said: "*Sacrifice and offering you did not desire, but a body you prepared for me; with burnt offerings and sin offerings you were not pleased. Then I said, 'Here I am— it is written about me in the scroll— I have come to do your will, O God.'*"

Jesus continually referred to God as his Father. The relationship that formed the Godhead was all-important. The intimacy that existed between them was an important matter. When Jesus prayed, it was to the

Father, not to "God." He often referred to "my Father." Consider the love and tenderness, the protection and security, provided to a child by the father. All this was illustrated by Jesus' references to his relationship with the Father. The Son has always been at the Father's side (John 1:18).

We must remember he was the *firstborn* among many brothers.[24] He never fails to also add references to *your* Father and *our* Father, carefully including us in this intimacy.[25] The family nature of God's community is inherent in all Jesus taught and said. Peter writes, *"Praise be to the God and Father of our Lord Jesus Christ! In his great mercy he has given us new birth into a living hope through the resurrection of Jesus Christ from the dead."*[26]

There are not separate sonships, one for Christ and one for the rest of us. As Milt Rodrigruez explains,

> There is only the one sonship of Jesus Christ. You and I, as believers, all participate and live in that one sonship. We are only God's sons through and in Christ. . . . We have no independent relationship with God apart from Christ. He *is* the Relationship. . . . So *we* can call God our Father just as He calls God His father, because we share the same Sonship. And that Sonship is Christ![27]

The centrality of Christ

The centrality of the Son in revealing the Godhead must be fully grasped to experience the fullness of operating within a Christ's Basic Body. To teach that the believer first receives Christ and then separately receives the Holy Spirit violates the teaching of Scripture. When we receive Christ, we have the Father and the Spirit. When we receive more of the Spirit through his many fillings, we are receiving more of Christ and the Father.[28] When the Spirit fills us, he is filling us with the Father and the person of Christ. His filling is not exclusively a filling of himself independently of the Father and the Son.

As each person of the Godhead functions, all participate. The triune identities have different roles, but none operates separately from the other two. The role of Christ, incarnated within Jesus, becomes the supreme revelation of the Godhead. He reveals the kingdom reign of God over all creation.[29] He does this not with words but with the amazing power of God that controls the sea, raises the dead, and multiplies loaves and fishes. What some refer to as the "power of the Holy Spirit" is identical to the "power of Christ." They are one and the same.

Indeed, it is Christ himself who is specifically mentioned as the one who inspired the writing of the prophets, which is also attributed in the second passage to the Holy Spirit:

> 1 Peter 1:10, 11: *Concerning this salvation, the prophets, who spoke of the grace that was to come to you, searched intently and with the greatest care, trying to find out the time and circumstances to which* the Spirit of Christ in them *was pointing when he predicted the sufferings of Christ and the glories that would follow* (emphasis mine).

> 2 Peter 1:21: *For prophecy never had its origin in the will of man, but men spoke from God as they were* carried along by the Holy Spirit (emphasis mine).

The role of the Holy Spirit is to *supplement* the revelation of the Godhead, to be the "one called alongside to help," to "guide us into all truth." As Jesus said, the Spirit will *"teach you all things, and will remind you of everything I have said to you."*[30] Note that the teaching of Christ Jesus is recalled through the Spirit's activity. The supreme revelation of the Godhead is always, first of all, the work of the Son, the Christ.

To summarize, God thinks and acts as community, not as separate individuals. God is community; therefore he thinks and acts corporately. We are self-centered, not community-based. Because of our propensity to individualism, we tend to define the Godhead as separate entities.

In South Africa, I attended a cell group in Cape Town. I joined in singing, "Jesus, I love You, I worship and adore You . . ." The song's further verses focused on "Father, I love You," and "Spirit, I love You . . ." I was struck by the way the Christ, the Anointed One, the *Son*, was missing from the song. As I pondered this, we went on to sing two more songs about Jesus. I have absolutely no problem in singing worship songs focused on Jesus, our Lord and Savior. Nevertheless, I realized that in nearly all sermons, songs, and conversations we stopped with Jesus.

After the worship time, I asked, "Do you ever sing about the Christ who dwelled in Jesus that also dwells in you?" Not a person knew of a song that emphasized this great truth. The fact of the matter is that today's song writers seem to ignore the position of the Son, the Christ, and focus only on the incarnated Jesus. I asked the group, "Whose Spirit is in our midst as we gather here? Is it the Spirit of Jesus, or the Spirit of Christ?"

Blank stares revealed the confusion in the group. We entered into a discussion about the eternal Christ who existed from before the foundations of the world and who will reign over the coming Kingdom. As we reviewed the scriptures that pointedly teach that Christ dwells in us and together we compose His present body on the earth, it was obvious none of them had digested this central teaching of scripture.

I reminded them about the two who walked to Emmaus with the resurrected Jesus without recognizing Him. As He expounded the Old Testament scriptures He asked, *"Ought not Christ to have suffered these things, and to enter into his glory?"* Even as Jesus' identity was hidden to them, so we today seem to live in ignorance about the Christ who lives in us. A cell group that does not understand the importance of communing with the indwelling Christ is cut off from His headship and His leadership.

But how will they *learn* of the position of Christ in their midst? If our frequently repeated praise songs mention only the historical Jesus, how will believers grasp it is the eternal Spirit of Christ who dwelled in Jesus who now dwells in them?

How many *sermons* from the pulpits of our churches have ever expounded on the position of Christ the Son, commissioned by the Godhead, to inhabit His new body? Ignorance of the truth must be laid at the feet of leadership that itself speaks only and always of Jesus and never of the Christ who was incarnated in Jesus.

Equipping materials for cell groups often ignore this crucial central truth. Thus, the cell is introduced to a Christless lifestyle, in some ways a body without a head. This flies in the face of all Paul taught!

Peter Snyman grasped this truth during my time with the Lighthouse community in Cape Town and wrote a song we sing together at the beginning of every worship service at the TOUCH Family here in Houston:

> *The Christ who dwells in me greets the Christ who dwells in you,*
> *Be welcome here, be welcome here.*
> *For when He works in me He uses one like you,*
> *Be welcome here, be welcome here.*
> *For we are His body, and He is our life,*
> *When He gives instructions, between us there's no strife.*
> *The Christ who dwells in me greets the Christ who dwells in you,*
> *Be welcome here, be welcome here.*

Focusing on the Holy Spirit's presence alone hampers a cell group from understanding their mission, ministering the gifts of Christ to one another and establishing their authentic identity as the literal body of Christ. We must create a sense of urgency to examine every cell group launched without this clear teaching, for they are probably all man-made groups and not Christ-directed bodies.

There is a heaven and earth difference between a group that communes with the indwelling Christ and one that does not! The comment made by the two men on the Emmaus Road was, "*Did not our heart burn within us while He talked to us while on the way, and while He opened to us the scriptures?"* A Christ-empowered group experiences "heartburn" on a regular basis! I have experienced such a community frequently. One problem it often has is a desire to go on, and on, and on, long past the "scheduled" closing time. It is a time of glorious communion with the King. Worship emanates from anyone and everyone in the group rather than a "worship leader." And, like Peter Snyman, songs of the heart are often crafted on the spot.

I have heard somewhere that the passage in Philippians 2:4-11 was sung as a hymn by the early bodies of Christ. Did Paul's words get set to music in a cell? Great truth about Christ Jesus is set into these words, to be repeated by His present body:

Look not every man on his own things, but every man also on the things of others. Let this mind be in you, which was also in Christ Jesus: Who, being in the form of God, thought it not robbery to be equal with God: But made himself of no reputation, and took upon him the form of a servant, and was made in the likeness of men: And being found in fashion as a man, he humbled himself, and became obedient unto death, even the death of the cross. Wherefore God also hath highly exalted him, and given him a name which is above every name: That at the name of Jesus every knee should bow, of things in heaven, and things in earth, and things under the earth; And that every tongue should confess that Jesus Christ is Lord, to the glory of God the Father. (KJV)

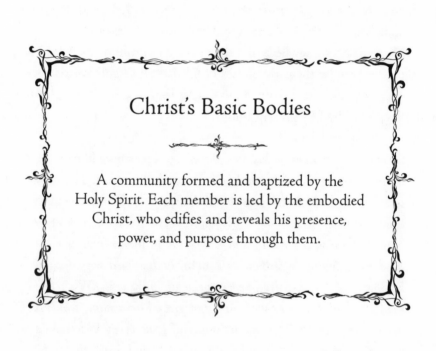

Christ's Basic Bodies

A community formed and baptized by the
Holy Spirit. Each member is led by the embodied
Christ, who edifies and reveals his presence,
power, and purpose through them.

chapter eight

The Four Tasks
of the Eternal Christ

When you have lifted up the Son of Man, then you will know that I am [the one I claim to be] and that I do nothing on my own but speak just what the Father has taught me. The one who sent me is with me; he has not left me alone, for I always do what pleases him. (John 8:28-30)

I was powerfully impacted when I found E. Stanley Jones' book *The Unshakable Kingdom and the Unchanging Person.* He explains that beyond the temporary kingdoms of this world, God is establishing his powerful eternal reign through his Son, who is the same *"yesterday, today, and forever."* These two powerful themes seem to be lost in the untidiness of Bible studies and sermons today. As a result, we sing songs about Jesus that do not adequately express the nature of the Christ, the Son, the one history revolves around . . . far beyond the thirty-three years he lived in Jesus on the earth.

Christ, the "Sent One," had four assignments to fulfill on behalf of the Godhead. The four assignments were in three stages. In the first stage, he descended to earth to fulfill the first two assignments: the prophesied kingdom would be revealed and the atonement for sin would be paid.

In the second stage, requiring thousands of years, Christ would also indwell his new body—the *ekklesia*—to penetrate the earth with his witness. The Holy Spirit calls forth those who are to belong to this new body. Christ's presence then prepares them for their tasks in the second stage.

A future and last stage of one thousand years will establish the reign of Christ over all the kingdoms of this earth. Upon completion of that reign, he will surrender his completed work to the Father and the kingdom of God will exist eternally.

IN JESUS, CHRIST INTRODUCED
THE UNSHAKABLE KINGDOM

The eternal plan of God was formed far in advance of the creation act. He will, at the end of the plan, reign over all he created. Everything will express him fully and completely. There will then be an eternal kingdom of God. It will be preceded by the lengthy activity of the kingdom of Christ, who will reign *"until he has put all his enemies under his feet."*[1]

The complete control of the universe was seen by Daniel, the Old Testament prophet: *"In the time of those kings, the God of heaven will set up a kingdom that will never be destroyed, nor will it be left to another people. It will crush all those kingdoms and bring them to an end, but it will itself endure forever."*[2]

The kingdom of God was the theme of all Jesus' teachings. In Matthew 4:23 we are told, *"Jesus went throughout Galilee, teaching in their synagogues, preaching the good news of the kingdom, and healing every disease and sickness among the people."*[3] The parables in Matthew are described as *"the mysteries of the kingdom of heaven."*[4]

Satan sought to control Jesus by offering him *"all the kingdoms of this world and their splendor,"*[5] not knowing that all of them would in the future become *"the kingdom of our Lord and of his Christ."*[6] The evil one would soon discover his kingdoms were being invaded by kingdom yeast through the coming of Christ.[7]

This reign of Christ was introduced not with words but with power. The miracles performed by Jesus were demonstrations of this supernatural reign. John the Baptist prophesied, *"The time is fulfilled, and the kingdom of God is at hand."*[8] When John came to the end of his life, he sent word to Jesus, asking for assurance that Jesus was the one who was to come. Jesus' response pointed to the miracles as proof that the kingdom had truly arrived.[9]

When Jesus sent out the disciples, they were ordered to proclaim the kingdom of God not with words but by healing the sick, cleansing lepers, raising the dead, and casting out demons. Because this was to be the proof of the kingdom's presence, he told them not to focus on funds or clothes to give away. The kingdom must come with the demonstration of power.[10] E. Stanley Jones wrote:

> Can we find any better illustration and meaning of the kingdom of God than in the person of Jesus Christ? He made himself and the Kingdom one—'auto basileia'—himself the kingdom. Would you want or could you imagine a better order than an order in which the spirit of Jesus Christ pervades, guides, and illustrates?. . . Is it good news to learn that the kingdom of God and Jesus are both called the Way?. . . An African explorer was being guided through a tractless jungle. He began to have doubts and said to his guide: "Is this the way?" The guide responded: "There is no way—I am the way." Does it mean anything to you that Jesus, the Person, and the Kingdom, the order, are both the Way?[11]

Christ brings his kingdom; the kingdom is the work of Christ. However, when we describe the kingdom, we are describing Christ. He is our righteousness, our wisdom, our holiness, our peace, our life. Only where he reigns does the kingdom exist. Where he does not reign the kingdom does not exist.

Christ indwells us. He does more than dispense to us qualities or gifts we need; he resides in us as the source of all power. The Christ who dwells in us is limitless and inexhaustible. He is the King of the kingdom, the one who reigns in the world today. Everything else pales before the reality of the King ruling over his kingdom.

Christ taught me that truth in a special way. I was directing a crusade in Dayton, Ohio. The stated preacher announced he was leaving before the final service, the climax for the meetings. Three TV stations would carry the stadium event statewide. Eight hours before the meeting, the sponsoring pastors met and assigned to me the task of preaching that night. In the afternoon, I feverishly rehearsed the message in an empty house loaned to me for sermon preparation. I did not relish preaching to ten thousand people with a massive TV viewing audience; it scared me to death! I "preached" my sermon to the mirror in the dining room and the bathroom.

The more I prepared, the weaker I felt inside. Finally I knelt and prayed, "Lord, give me your power!" He responded, "Sorry, I can't trust you with such power. Remember, I did not promise power in my commission for you to make disciples. Instead, I said, 'All power is given unto *me*, and I am with *you*.'" I then realized I was only a channel for the Christ who lived in me. His indwelling presence was the power—I was only his carrier. That night he spoke through me and I had no anxiety at all! The presence of Christ was manifested and many were drawn to him. Manfred Haller writes,

> God needs to deal drastically with us—so drastically that we let go of our own notions, until we see things from His perspective. Then shall Christ become real to us. . . . Begin seeing Christ behind everything. When you finally understand that Christ is everything you need, then you will have truly become Christocentric. Then you will share with the Father the most precious thing He has—His Son. Christ will become your only perspective, your only hope, your only possession, and your only interest.[12]

Entry into the kingdom takes place when Christ enters our lives. The expression of the kingdom is then done not with words alone but with his power being manifested. Thus, when *"all are prophesying"*[13] the unbeliever sees the kingdom, his reign, and cries out, "God is really among you!"[14] Our proclamation is done simply by revealing the presence and power of Christ Jesus. We are to reveal the King is among us and this is done when his power is manifested through us.

IN JESUS, CHRIST BECAME
THE ATONING SACRIFICE

Oh, can it be, upon a tree, the Savior died for me?
My soul is thrilled, my heart is filled, to think He died for me![15]

Our decision to reject Jesus Christ's claims of ownership over us caused his suffering at Calvary. Martin Luther did not understand that as a Catholic priest. When he became aware of the meaning of the crucifixion, he knelt before the carved crucifix with Christ hanging on it in the chapel and sobbed, "My God! My God! For me! For me!"

When I was in the second grade, a little Jewish boy returned to the schoolroom after recess, wiping a bloody nose. I asked, "What happened to you?" He replied, "Those boys beat me up because I am a Jew and they said the Jews killed Jesus."

How wrong they were! It was my sin, your sin, and the sins of mankind that caused his substitutionary death.

From the moment Adam needed a redeemer, he knew there was the promise of one. From the prophecy of Genesis 3:16 forward, humans have been aware that the Redeemer would come. By faith, Old Testament people looked forward to their Redeemer; by faith, those since Calvary accept the great event for their eternal salvation.

The Transfiguration experience was a special time in the life of Jesus. Moses and Elijah discussed with him his impending death.[16] The one who knew no sin would face its judgment; the thought of it caused Jesus to sweat like drops of blood.[17] The apostle Paul saw the death of Christ as the ultimate illustration to teach us to *"look not only to your own interests, but also to the interests of others."*[18] The direct application of how Christ paid the ultimate price to look after our interests is the way we are to understand our looking after the interests of others.

The future Calvary event was continually forecast in Israel's rituals. The symbolical lamb without spot or blemish was sacrificed for centuries, beginning with Abel's sacrifice.[19] The prediction was prophesied by Isaiah 742 years before Calvary.[20] The cry of John the Baptist was *"Look, the Lamb of God, who takes away the sin of the world!"*[21]

Among the New Age teachings found today, many ridicule the teaching of Calvary by stating they cannot accept that a loving God would kill his own son. They do not understand that God did not kill his Son; *we did!* It was our self-centered decision to steal ourselves from his rightful ownership that caused him to atone for our sin.

As was predicted by Peter, the cross is *"A stone of stumbling and a rock of offense."*[22]

After I produced and aired a radio message about the crucifixion, I received a phone call from a high-ranking military officer in the War College in Carlisle, Pennsylvania, asking me to visit with him. He sneered, "Your teaching about the blood of Jesus doesn't satisfy me!" I replied, "Sir, it was never meant to satisfy you. It was meant to satisfy God, and that is all that matters."

Blood is *not* merely symbolic for death when we are speaking of Christ's Atonement. God's law demands death *and* the shedding of blood for remission of sin (Lev. 17:11; Ezekiel 18:4; Romans 6:23; Hebrews 9:22). The Old Testament sacrifices depicted how the Lord Jesus Christ would pay the price for sin. The blood of the O.T. sacrifices did not merely depict Christ's death; it depicted Christ's *blood*. His death alone could not save us; His blood was required. In Romans 5:9-10 we see the two together. Verse 9 says we are justified *"by his blood,"* and verse 10 says we are reconciled *"by his death."* Any view that confuses the blood of Christ with His death is incomplete. Both are necessary.[23]

The blood of the cross is for God; the cross itself is for you. Paul said, "I have been crucified with Christ."[24] When your agenda is put to death at the cross, you will find the risen Christ living in you.

IN HIS NEW BODY,
CHRIST PENETRATES ALL NATIONS IN ALL AGES

We have come to the mission of Christ extending through the centuries. How did Christ intend for his command in Matthew 28:18-20 to be fulfilled? His third assignment on behalf of the Godhead is outlined:

> *Then Jesus came to them and said, "All authority in heaven and on earth has been given to me. Therefore go and make disciples of all nations, baptizing them in the name of the Father and of the Son and of the Holy Spirit, and teaching them to obey everything I have commanded you. And surely I am with you always, to the very end of the age."*

An institutional view of the church presents us with a problem as we read this passage. Its lifestyle fails to provide the structure needed to fulfill the task of the "called-out ones":[25]

1. Christ's presence will continually empower as he dwells within them.
2. Since Christ has all authority in heaven and earth, his new body will exercise it.
3. In his new body, Christ will penetrate every culture.
4. Converts will receive Christ's entrance into their lives, causing the kingdoms of this world to be further invaded by the kingdom of God.
5. His ministry while dwelling in us is to "*make* disciples." The term "make" means to "cause all cultures to experience Christ fully."

His assignment is the transformation of cultures by the transformation of people in them. Thus, the Chinese and the Spanish and the English will leave behind their separateness and become kingdom people. When Christ reigns, there is *"neither Jew nor Greek, slave nor free, male nor female."*[26] Churches practice spiritual apartheid by becoming ethnic associations in multicultural communities. This is a great tragedy to be corrected.[27] (We will consider this further in a future chapter.)

What does "teaching all things" *require?* Teaching "all things" as Jesus commanded cannot be done by instructing people in a classroom. How *do* we teach "all things"? Certainly not in one twenty-minute sermon a week! Nor by a weekly Bible study. Todd A. Brown, Small Group Minister in a West Texas church, shares:

> We have a Chinese house church leader living in a house on the church property. She is a refugee and was smuggled out of China a couple of months ago because of persecution. Of her 13 years as a believer, (12 as an evangelist and leader) she has been in prison 3 times for a total of 6 years. She led a large (multiple thousands) network of one of the 8 major movements. Because of her influence she was tortured multiple times.
>
> The first time she shared her testimony it was different than I expected. It was only later that I realized why. She told us about how they shackled her feet. They were so swollen and bruised that the cuffs cut into her ankles. They hurt so badly she asked the Lord to let her die. Then, and I quote, "I remembered that they had hurt Jesus' feet and it was all right." On another occasion they melted plastic bags on her hands and then electrocuted her fingers for long periods of time. How did she endure such torture? I quote again, "I remembered that they had hurt Jesus' hands and I was able to endure." Then they

stripped her naked and paraded her around the prison. This was the only point in her story when she faltered. The shame of the experience was so great it reached into that room with power. How did she keep going? You will not be surprised at her response: "I thought about how they had stripped Jesus and paraded him through the streets and that made it okay." At every turn her comfort was her identification with Jesus.

I have thought about this so much. In my mind I imagine the response most believers I know would have to hardship and suffering. There are many who would testify to God's ministering presence, but I don't think there are as many who would connect their suffering so directly to Jesus and receive sustaining comfort. I wonder if there is a connection between her Christ-centered way of thinking and the explosion of the church she was a part of from one family to more than 100,000.

This past week she taught our small group leaders about their organization and administration. She said they only have one training meeting a year for their house church leaders. These leaders are all vocational. They have day jobs. Their training meeting lasts for 45 days. What do they study? What is their curriculum? They spend a month and a half every year studying the life of Christ together for 8 hours a day. This is the foundation for ministry for the rest of the year.

One of our leaders asked her how they could take a month and half and still support their families. She didn't seem to understand the question and then answered it like we were biblically illiterate. She said very patiently and sweetly, "Jesus said that if we seek first the kingdom of God that all of that would be taken care of—and it is!"

In our generation, there is a desperate need to realize that the eternal Christ must complete his work by forming his new bodies into

CONTINUOUS PERSONAL DEVELOPMENT (CPD)

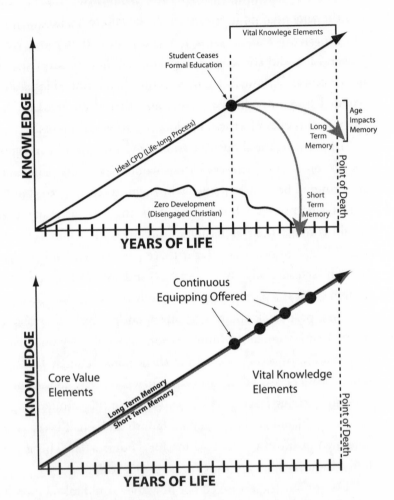

small communities flexible enough to penetrate every culture in an area. Their task is not only to share a message we call the "plan of salvation," but also to reveal his kingdom and presence manifested in them.

The fulfilling of the Great Commission requires much investment in post-conversion experiences. Disciples are not just "born again." They are being formed by the patient labor of body members who walk together and share, experiencing edification and his power and presence.

Harold Weitz, pastor of the Little Falls Christian Centre in South Africa, has used the term "Continuous Personal Development" to express the need for all believers to perpetually expand their knowledge of life in the kingdom of God. His top graph points out that discipleship is a lifetime process. If little or no attention is given to the constant equipping of all believers throughout their lifetimes, vital knowledge is lost. He is a stickler for providing continuous personal development (bottom graph) for all of his members. After training them in a three year equipping "college," they are then sent out to plant new cell churches in the region. He averages one new church plant every month by developing his members. He has even videotaped all the lectures for distribution on iPods so they can be readily available to students.

Teaching "all things" requires Christ's new body to reveal his life and acts to each new believer. They must be folded into a community to be taught through observation and life sharing experiences, not just lectures.

The anointing bestowed on Jesus empowered him to focus on areas of man's brokenness that cannot be solved by human devices. We seldom consider the amazing event that took place in the synagogue in Nazareth. It was just a regular Friday gathering of the men of the village. According to custom, there were seven readers every Sabbath. The first was a priest, the second a Levite. Then five Israelites were randomly selected from the audience.[28] Jesus was chosen. He unrolled the scroll to the next passage. He did not select it; it was marked by a red ribbon indicating the next passage to be read aloud in the meetings. Isaiah had recorded his job description 742 years before, which Jesus read:

The Spirit of the Lord is on me, because he has anointed me to preach good news to the poor. He has sent me to proclaim freedom for the prisoners and recovery of sight for the blind, to release the oppressed, to proclaim the year of the Lord's favor.[29]

Jesus—the Christ—had a special mission. It was to "preach," to "proclaim," to "recover," to "release," to declare that the kingdom of God has come to fulfill what was, in Jewish life, an occurrence that took place only every fifty years, the Year of Jubilee (the "year of the Lord's favor").[30] On that year, property returned to its original owner. Thus, the "good news for the poor" was their inheritance was restored. Slaves regained their liberty. It is as though Jesus is proclaiming, "The kingdom of God is here. Every day is a day of power to bring deliverance from the pains of sickness and oppression."

He lived in such a way that those who followed him adopted his values and his lifestyle. He was a friend of drunks and sinners. He healed the blind, raised the dead, and in many ways demonstrated his anointing by his activities. Moreover, he modeled for his new body members, the "called-out ones," how he expected them to carry him within to fulfill his final mission. It would require them to be among the people who need his presence and power. Consider this comment made by Todd Brown:

> He became God in the flesh, so those who are filled with Him will also care about the poor and outcast, penetrating their world . . . The humanity of Jesus is what shapes how we live. I know many western believers who accept the divine atonement but dismiss the life and ministry of Jesus as irrelevant. Jesus did what he did because he was "God." I can't "keep in step with the Spirit" or "Do only what I see my Father doing" and go into an unreached neighborhood or heart because I am not "fully God" like he was. The power of the Chinese woman's story to me is not just that she is connected with the divine Christ, but with the human Jesus in his suffering. Her mindset is that if Jesus did it, so will I.[31]

Many Scriptures present Christ as the believer's model. Consider these passages (emphasis mine):

Romans 15:5, 6: *Now may the God of patience and comfort grant you to be like-minded toward one another,* according to Christ Jesus, *that you may with one mind and one mouth glorify the God and Father of our Lord Jesus Christ* (emphasis mine).

Philippians 2:5: *Let this mind be in you which was also* in Christ Jesus (*NKJV*, emphasis mine).

Hebrews 12:1, 2: *Therefore we also, since we are surrounded by so great a cloud of witnesses, let us lay aside every weight, and the sin which so easily ensnares us, and let us run with endurance the race that is set before us,* looking unto Jesus, *the author and finisher of our faith, who for the joy that was set before Him endured the cross, despising the shame, and has sat down at the right hand of the throne of God* (*NKJV*, emphasis mine).

1 Peter 2:20, 21: *For what credit is it if, when you are beaten for your faults, you take it patiently? But when you do good and suffer, if you take it patiently, this is commendable before God. For to this you were called,* because Christ also suffered for us, leaving us an example, that you should follow His steps (*NKJV*, emphasis mine).

1 John 2:6: *He who says he abides in Him ought himself also* to walk just as He walked (*NKJV*, emphasis mine).

The present work of Christ requires him to be transported by his new body to meet the people he has come to serve. Today's Christian community must reveal his presence and power. That is our only task.

THE CONSUMMATION OF CHRIST'S ASSIGNMENT IS TO FORM THE ETERNAL KINGDOM OF GOD

The twelve disciples did not at first grasp the teachings of Jesus about the kingdom. They expected him to overthrow the Roman government and establish a Jewish kingdom. For some of them, their motive for following him was to gain political position when he used his powers to overthrow the hated government. James and John even asked him for the two top spots.[32] Their own mother tried to manipulate Jesus on their behalf.[33]

They did not understand their role in the coming kingdom. They were not prepared to be servants. They wanted power. They needed to be groomed, to die to their agenda. Jesus saw the necessity of organizing an *ekklesia* with them, slowly preparing them for the time when they would serve in a world-conquering community.

His three years of "boot camp" with them were not quite enough. Close to the end of his life, they were still arguing about who would be the greatest among them when Jesus' kingdom was formed.[34] It took the death and resurrection of Christ to make them grasp what he had been telling them about the kingdom. Only then did they grasp the full impact of his teaching. They also would need the rest of their lifetimes to be prepared for kingdom service. For Peter, the training would include being crucified upside-down and for Paul to die a martyr's death. At the last Paul wrote:

> *I have fought the good fight, I have finished the race, I have kept the faith. Now there is in store for me the crown of righteousness, which the Lord, the righteous Judge, will award to me on that day—and not only to me, but also to all who have longed for his appearing.*[35]

In our culture, we expect instant gratification and rapid satisfaction of our goals. As we enter the kingdom, we are also promised a place of service in the future kingdom. It is crucial for us to recognize the link between our present "boot camp" experiences and that future time when we will reign with him. We must practice kingdom living *in this life* in preparation for our future reign with him *in the age to come*.

In this present age, every Christ's Basic Body should recognize we are all in "boot camp" for the time when the kingdom of Christ will replace the kingdoms of this earth. At that time, we will be required to serve him as he reigns over the earth.

Dissipating our lives in temporal activities is truly shortsighted when we realize that after less than a century of living now, we will serve him for *ten centuries* in the next period of his reign. At the launching of that era, Paul describes the time of judgment for all believers.[36] We will appear before a special judgment throne to determine whether we wasted our lives, building in this age with wood, hay, or straw, or whether we invested our years preparing ourselves for the future kingdom tasks.

Jesus was very blunt in his parable of the master who entrusted funds to his servants, requesting they invest them wisely. Burying one's talents in the ground did not sit well when the master returned!

Every Christian and every Christ's Basic Body has a responsibility to serve effectively *now* so that in his coming reign, we will be prepared to perform kingdom tasks. When we consider today's vast audiences of Christians who seldom pray, never share their faith and are not participants in a valid structure of authentic *ekklesia*, it is a dreadful thing to anticipate the future accounting at the judgment seat.

The "fire" that will consume the wood, hay, and straw is the *Shekinah* glory of God. When his glory judges our conduct, it will wither away! Such evaluation will leave the believer with only Christ as the reason to live in the future kingdom. Further, after ten centuries the Son will surrender his reign to the Father. In that time when all is consummated and the last vestiges of evil are eternally erased, we are told God will wipe away all tears from our eyes. It would seem some Christians who had their works on earth destroyed as wood, hay, and straw at the end of the millennium will finally be relieved of weeping over the mistakes made by the investment of life today.[37]

The New Testament writings are packed with prophecies of future events. The message of Jesus was clearly about future events. The early church lived anticipating the future events. The whispered word when Christians met in the midst of great persecution was *Maranatha* (The Master is coming).

Conclusion

The most sacred activity of the King of Kings in the world today takes place as he occupies Christ's Basic Bodies, the "called-out ones." The task of Christ is to so occupy them that in their experiences they will manifest his power: healing, restoring, and edifying them as members of his holy community. It will be in them and through them that Christ will function to reveal his presence to unbelievers and ungifted ones. All he does he will do through this source of his presence on the earth.

Further, the intimacy we are to experience here and now with him, learning to hear his voice, sensing his power flowing through us for ministry to others, is "boot camp" training for a coming age. We must not live in this age *for* this age, but rather realize this short experience on earth (lasting for less than a century) is designed to groom us to serve him then. Our redemption is not provided so we can go to heaven when we die. It is to prepare us to be instruments of Christ in his coming kingdom reign, to be blended into others so we live in the unity of his body.

We are God-formed communities, not man-made organizations. We are to learn how to know his voice, as sheep who hear their Shepherd. We are to experience his power flowing through us, revealing his invisible presence through supernatural evidences. We are to redeem the time, for as Paul reminds us,

What I mean, brothers and sisters in Christ, is that the time is short! From now on those who have wives should live as if they had none; those who mourn, as if they did not; those who are happy, as if they were not; those who buy something, as if it were not theirs to keep; those who use the things of the world, as if not engrossed in them. For this world in its present form is passing away.

(1 Corinthians 7:29-31)

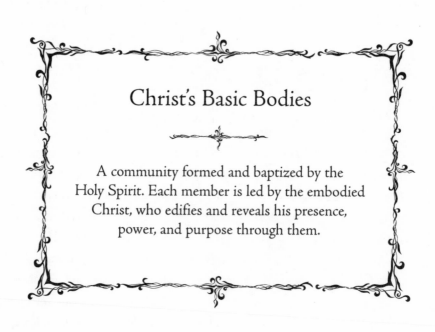

Christt's Basic Bodies

A community formed and baptized by the
Holy Spirit. Each member is led by the embodied
Christ, who edifies and reveals his presence,
power, and purpose through them.

Christ Inhabits His Called-Out Ones

He said to them: "It is not for you to know the times or dates the Father has set by his own authority. But you will receive power when the Holy Spirit comes on you; and you will be my witnesses in Jerusalem, and in all Judea and Samaria, and to the ends of the earth." . . . When the day of Pentecost came, they were all together in one place. Suddenly a sound like the blowing of a violent wind came from heaven and filled the whole house where they were sitting. They saw what seemed to be tongues of fire that separated and came to rest on each of them. All of them were filled with the Holy Spirit and began to speak in other tongues as the Spirit enabled them. Now there were staying in Jerusalem God-fearing Jews from every nation under heaven. When they heard this sound, a crowd came together in bewilderment, because each one heard them speaking in his own language. Utterly amazed, they asked: "Are not all these men who are speaking Galileans? Then how is it that each of us hears them in his own native language? Parthians, Medes and Elamites; residents of Mesopotamia, Judea and Cappadocia, Pontus and Asia, Phrygia and Pamphylia, Egypt and the parts of Libya near Cyrene; visitors from Rome (both Jews and converts to Judaism); Cretans and Arabs-we hear them declaring the wonders of God in our own tongues!" Amazed and perplexed, they asked one another, "What does this mean?   (Acts 1:7, 8; 2:1-12)

On the day of Pentecost, sleeping Jewish tourists filled the streets of Jerusalem. They traveled from many nations to attend this harvest-home celebration. It climaxed as the high priest waved two loaves of leavened, salted bread to the Lord in gratitude for sustaining Israel.

As dawn broke, a priest carrying a scythe and rope stepped between the prostrate people and passed through a gate in the city wall. In a special field where pure wheat was grown for this special event, he cut enough grain to form loaves of bread.

The loaves were fashioned exactly as ordered in Leviticus 23:17.[1] When the special moment arrived, all Jerusalem stood at attention. From the temple galleries, banners waved to notify those in the streets that the loaves were being waved. It was the moment when the day of Pentecost "had fully come."

In a wealthy man's large upper room, 120 of Jesus' followers were completing ten days of living in community. Observing Jesus' ascent into the clouds had impacted them deeply; they followed his instructions to remain together. They anticipated a gift Jesus had promised the Father would send to them.

Let's try to imagine what took place during those ten days. They had no agenda, no schedule. Perhaps one of them asked Peter, "What is our agenda? How long will we remain here?" Did Peter shrug his shoulders and say, "How long? Your guess is as good as mine. But I think I know the agenda: *The agenda is us!*"

They had one assignment: to become *one* in spirit and truth. That required ten intensive days of eating, sleeping, and sharing together. They must have formed groups as they recalled Jesus' words and deeds. He had spoken so many parables! What did they mean?

They listened to each story about the way the others had experienced Jesus. Hearts became transparent as family and personal matters were shared. There was weeping, laughing, hugging, singing. Jesus had prayed that his followers would be *one, in full accord.* That was their agenda.

On the tenth day, they were aware the two loaves would be waved in the temple. Perhaps some were even thinking about slipping into the crowd in the streets below.

Then it happened!

Although the sky was cloudless, a violent wind shook the whole house. They experienced tongues of fire that split apart to enter each one of them. *What was the substance forming those flames?*

It was not physical fire, for it did not scorch the hair of the 120. When it penetrated their bodies, did it bounce off their ribs and fly out through the walls? *No!* The streaming flames were the glory of God, called the *Shekinah* fire in Hebrew.[2] This presence remained within each person.

This was the same glory-fire Moses saw in a bush that was not consumed. It was the glory-fire Israel saw as God spoke from his pulpit at Mount Sinai and then led them through the wilderness, hovering above the tabernacle at night. It was the glory-fire that touched Isaiah's tongue as God asked, "Whom shall I send? And who will go for us?"[3]

It was also the *sending* glory fire Jeremiah experienced when he wrote: "*But if I say, 'I will not mention him or speak any more in his name,' his word is in my heart like a fire, a fire shut up in my bones. I am weary of holding it in; indeed, I cannot.*"[4]

The Spirit of God was the *Shekinah* fire. Jesus had promised they would soon receive the Holy Spirit: now, that fire was the presence of *Elohim*, the Creator. The Spirit of the Godhead was fashioning a special body with a baptism of his glory.

Amazing! The Creator who had taken the dust of the earth to form the first Adam and who had planted a seed in a Jewish girl, was the Creator once again. This event had been planned before the earth was created.

God's Holy Spirit was sealing their spirits by his own. They were being made *segullah*, his special treasure![5] The 120 became the first members of the "called-out ones," the *ekklesia*, the new body Christ would occupy. In this body he would go to all people in all generations, offering salvation and his kingdom reign. Jesus said, "*Surely I am with you always, to the very end of the age.*" The word for *with* is the Greek word *meta*, indicating Christ's presence supplying his divine power and aid.[6]

God's Holy Spirit created the new body for Christ. Christ's Basic Bodies were, and are, his special creation:

The body is a unit, though it is made up of many parts; and though all its parts are many, they form one body. So it is with Christ. For

we were all baptized by one Spirit into one body—whether Jews or
Greeks, slave or free—and we were all given the one Spirit to drink.[7]

In that upper room, Christ, the second Adam, married his new
bride. *Elohim* officiated at the wedding. He joined two to become one.
Because the 120 were "all in one accord," he had no difficulty joining
spiritual hands to feet, forming inward parts that would compose the
first of Christ's bodies. While we have no hard evidence that these 120
broke down into small groups to manifest Christ's Basic Bodies, it is
safe to assume that they did so because that was the pattern Jesus
practiced with them as he met with the twelve. There were about a
dozen of them, but this bride would soon be pregnant and would see
children added to the family. This bride and Groom then went to
celebrate their new union in the streets. Their emotions bubbled over
with holy anointing as they shouted to all, "He's back! He's back! The
Spirit who dwelled in Jesus is in us! Christ is here right now!"

These followers of Jesus had known Christ intimately as he
occupied the body of Jesus. As a wife can identify the sounds of her
husband even in the midst of her deepest sleep, the 120 recognized
Jesus Christ had inhabited them. They were now part of his special
dwelling place to serve him for centuries to come.

God was creatively at work in that upper room. The Creator *Elohim*
formed a spiritual body never before present on the earth. That new
body contained the King of the kingdom. In that body, Christ would
loose and bind on earth what is loosed and bound in heaven. *This bride*
would become the most sacred treasure of the Godhead. Through Christ, it
would contain all the fullness of the Godhead.[8] Peter would later
describe this body in his letter to them:

To God's elect, strangers in the world, scattered throughout Pontus,
Galatia, Cappadocia, Asia and Bithynia, who have been chosen
according to the foreknowledge of God the Father, through the

sanctifying work of the Spirit, for obedience to Jesus Christ and sprinkling by his blood.[9]

Consider these insights about what happened to the 120:

The *Shekinah* created Christ's Basic Bodies in her outward form and her inner life.

The outward form God created was not to form a large assembly. He took the first 120 and immediately baptized them into Christ's Basic Bodies. The *ekklesia* might expand to be a worldwide community, but the Spirit's baptisms would shape a few people into a community for Christ to inhabit.

How many arms and legs can a single body contain? Did not Jesus say *"For where two or three come together in my name, there am I with them"*?[10] Man thinks significance increases by the size of a gathering. This was not Jesus' pattern. When the five thousand tried to follow him, he went far away from them. Instead, he chose to live among twelve men. His parables were for a few, not all. He focused on intimate and accountable relationships, not the masses.

We have it all wrong! Today, churches focus on the large gathering. The bigger the crowd, the more successful the church. This flies in the face of what God intended for his kingdom subjects. The "small group" movement is a secondary priority, seen as optional or supportive to the large assembly. Satan himself is the one who has duped us into thinking that our first priority is to build a huge congregation and call it "church."

This was not what Jesus endorsed! He knew the kingdom of God could not exist where masses gathered for self-enrichment. When the crowds followed him after they were fed, he went away.[11] When they still followed him, he rebuked them saying, *"You are looking for me, not because you saw miraculous signs but because you ate the loaves and had your fill.*[12]

God organized the Israelites into groups of ten.[13] This is the size of community, where people can be accountable to and for each other. A terrible deception rests upon the way churches operate today. Billions of dollars have been spent erecting ornate or expansive buildings in the name of the Lord.

We count "nickels and noses" to evaluate success in the Christian movement. Have we forgotten how angry God became when David considered his personal significance by numbering the people?[14]

When the focus is changed from gathering large crowds to forming Christ's Basic Bodies, there will be awesome growth. Around the world today where basic cell churches exist, the head count of those who combine as Christ's bodies is awesome: 160,000 and more in the Ivory Coast, 130,000 or more in tiny El Salvador. Yet the focus in every case is not how large the public meetings are, but how many cells of fifteen or less exist. In Jakarta, Indonesia, AbbaLove's cell groups gather on Sundays to worship in more than seventy separate gatherings, scattered in buildings miles apart in a city of over 13 million people. Because of political oppression, they have not been able to build or own property. It has kept them from owning facilities, causing them to grow faster by focusing on cell groups.

When I train church planters, my first strong recommendation is that they focus exclusively on forming Christ's Basic Bodies and resist gathering for a Sunday worship service until they reach 120, or twelve groups. Until that time, any clustering of groups for training or worship can be done in a small space. This keeps them from falling back into old patterns of "bigger is better" and losing sight of what is most important.

The outward form also shaped the inner life.

Every single one of the 120 manifested supernatural evidence that Christ came to indwell their lives. All of them were overcome with joy in the streets as they shared the good news that Christ had returned. Later in his first letter to the Corinthians, Paul would use the term *hekastos*, (each one) to describe the spiritual empowerment manifested by all members of the Christ's Basic Bodies.[15] The outward form would reveal the joy and sensitivity of the indwelling King; her inner life would experience the intimacy of a bride with her husband, a life filled with unbridled love.

One of the contrasts between the body of Christ then and now is the lack of experiencing the kingdom. Words of an old chorus said, "I was there when it happened, and I ought to know," but for many being "there" is now a reference to a gathering where a public announcement is made for people to "follow Christ." Without an authentic invasion of Christ into a life, there is no foundation to build upon. Evangelistic invitations for people to "surrender to Christ" may not even describe salvation as Christ and the Holy Spirit taking charge of that life forever.

In an authentic community, all will manifest Christ's presence and power. The fact that few cell groups or small groups today experience this total participation of "all prophesying" indicates we have a long way to go.

Christ's Basic Bodies were the work of God, not the disciples.

When the tongues fell, the twelve disciples of Jesus were not singled out to receive a "first wave" before the rest in the room were touched. There was only one wave. All experienced the same thing simultaneously. None among the 120 considered themselves to be organized by the twelve disciples! They knew they were the creation of God, not man. In their understanding, each Christ's Basic Body was the work of God. As the ground was level for all at the foot of the cross, it was level again when the fire fell. It would take Satan many generations to install men who would build significance for themselves in the movement.

It is hard for us to grasp the unity that was present in that upper room! God is no respecter of persons. The greatest among them was to be seen by him as the servant of all. They would all see themselves as slaves of the King, possessing no personal property except that entrusted to them by the Master.

The miraculous was at center stage.

They experienced the miraculous, the creation of God. Not only had Christ risen from the dead and ascended into the clouds as they watched, but now he had returned to live within them. Imagine the inner sensations they experienced as his life flooded their personalities with his presence! They were all commissioned to be apostles. They saw things outside the natural order and knew they would forever live in a kingdom that is not of this world.

Because they experienced this miracle in the beginning, their whole mind and will was on Christ. Their very existence was based on doing his work. The miraculous was at the center stage from the outset and energized everything they would do.

Faith became the focus of their lives. They immediately took Christ's Basic Bodies to the neighborhoods. They were swamped by new converts: three thousand converts responded to Peter's explanation. Each Christ's Basic Body would absorb them. They moved from house to house, all in one accord. The Lord added to their number *daily* those who were being saved.[16] By Acts 4:4, the number of men alone had grown to five thousand.

Amazing! They had no seminaries to train them. They had no Bibles to study. They had no senior pastors. The apostles were not reigning over them, but rather equipping them. *They had Christ, and Christ alone!* They shared the memories of Jesus with those who shared their meals:

> *They devoted themselves to the apostles' teaching and to the fellowship, to the breaking of bread and to prayer. Everyone was filled with awe, and many wonders and miraculous signs were done by the apostles. All the believers were together and had everything in common. Selling their possessions and goods, they gave to anyone as he had need. Every day they continued to meet together in the temple courts.[17] They broke bread in their homes and ate together*

with glad and sincere hearts, praising God and enjoying the favor of all the people. And the Lord added to their number daily those who were being saved.[18]

Adolf Schlatter, a respected Evangelical theologian and professor writes,

The disciples never confined God's activity to the miraculous, but brought even ordinary events under his sovereignty, never imagining them to be an obstacle to fellowship with him. Miracles were highly valued and thankfully acknowledged whenever they occurred. They were a powerful confirmation of faith, at any rate for the believers themselves. . . . The Church's confidence in her miraculous illumination never displaced the need for mental effort but on the contrary enhanced it. Her consciousness of her supernatural powers, so far from hindering the adaptation of her activity to the environment in which she found herself, turned it into a duty. In all her life, even in the natural side, the Church looked up to God, who in his almighty power reveals himself in miracle to those who serve him.[19]

Their prayer life focused on the indwelling Christ.

As you come to him, the living Stone—rejected by men but chosen by God and precious to him—you also, like living stones, are being built into a spiritual house to be a holy priesthood, offering spiritual sacrifices acceptable to God through Jesus Christ.[20]

It is significant to note that when they moved from house to house as Christ's Basic Bodies, the first thing they did was to break bread as a sign of their unity, and the second thing they did was pray. They were aware that Christ was in their midst, not in heaven above. Thus, their prayers were directed inwardly to him, not upwardly. Communion with Christ was a special event when body members gathered. Schlatter continues with this:

> From prayer in the Spirit, compounded as it was of confession and adoration, the Church looked for two very different results. That the Spirit is the giver of the Word was recognized from the difference between the Word and ordinary speech. The worshipper sought new modes of expression, surpassing everyday language, for the powerful emotions that moved him. His prayer took him out of his natural environment, made him look within himself and lifted him up· towards God, alone, a solitary being, unconnected with others. But on a different view, prayer in the Spirit removed all the barriers between speakers and hearers, creating fellowship between them, which was plain for all to see. In this way, according to the Lucan account, speaking in tongues contributed to the rise of the Church in Jerusalem.[21]

The disciples learnt to see the Spirit at work throughout their spiritual life. They saw him at work in their testimony to the Messiahship of Jesus, when they discerned in Christ crucified the "Lord of glory" and in him who lived in the flesh the presence of the Word of God. They saw him in their prayer, which filled them with joy and certainty and which, when it broke out into speaking with tongues, transcended the limits of normal thought and speech. They saw him at work in the insight they acquired into hidden mysteries, in their victorious onslaught on the powers of destruction, and in their speech, wherein they spoke as prophets in the name of God, revealing to the Church his will.[22]

They possessed a strong commitment to future kingdom events.

Peter was present in that upper room. Much later, he would write:

In his great mercy he has given us new birth into a living hope through the resurrection of Jesus Christ from the dead, and into an inheritance that can never perish, spoil or fade—kept in heaven for you, who through faith are shielded by God's power until the coming of the salvation that is ready to be revealed in the last time.[23]

The return of Jesus would take place "in the last time." Had he not taught that no one but the Father knew exactly when that would be?[24] The expected return was always on their minds. A favorite greeting was "Maranatha!" (The Master is coming!). Their ability to invest all their present hours in that which would produce fruit for the coming kingdom shaped all their values.

Since the kingdom was coming, investments were sold to equalize the support of fellow body members. Widows were given provisions. Their focus on the future made it possible for believers to hold treasures in their hands, not their hearts. Peter reminded them that the elements would dissolve with fervent heat.[25]

"Living today for tomorrow" was a core value! The kingdom was everything and the present life was unimportant. They had witnessed the resurrected Christ so death was not an end for them. There would be no losing possessions by dying. Paul would remind them of the future treasures awaiting them, now being prepared for them by Jesus Christ—heavenly places!

The revolution

I will never forget my first visit to China after the Cultural Revolution ended. In a village near Macau, I saw a church building erected by Methodist missionaries many years before. It now served as a factory where sewing machines were made. Nearby was a Buddhist temple filled with grain; it had been converted into a warehouse. The communists had destroyed all religious institutions and their buildings, eliminating physical reminders of the past to enhance their new society.

Little did they know that Christ's Basic Bodies would flourish in this society. From a small percentage of the Chinese under the old religious systems, an explosion of faith took place. Without buildings, seminaries, *even Bibles*, the kingdom of God was planted like yeast in the flour of communism. It cannot be stamped out. For every person arrested, tortured, or beaten, a hundred others flourished.

Do you realize how far the Christian movement has drifted through the centuries? Further, do you realize what it will require for the Holy Spirit to form authentic Christ's Basic Bodies?

In the chapters that follow, we will examine what must take place if we are to become bodies indwelled by Christ. Doing so will necessitate breaking free from religious structures and a commitment to traditions. That is why I wonder if God's creation of the last days church will have to begin with some far-flung tribal group in a desert place in Kenya, where unspoiled humans will not copy wrong patterns. Or, will he begin with the twenty million in America who have—with disillusionment—dropped out of all religious systems but are still searching for reality?

It seems impossible for those who have climbed religious ladders to backtrack to the ground and start over. The need for Christ's Basic Bodies to be revealed is crucial. Surely the Holy Spirit is even now searching for those he will select and baptize to become his bodies, empowering them to focus on community, edification, and becoming true witnesses of his internal presence.

What do you think? Is it *wrong* to propagate a religious system in which major concentration is given to public services and where small groups become optional activities to keep believers busy until we can present the next large event? Imagine the radical revolution that will be needed to stop all we are doing to get it right.

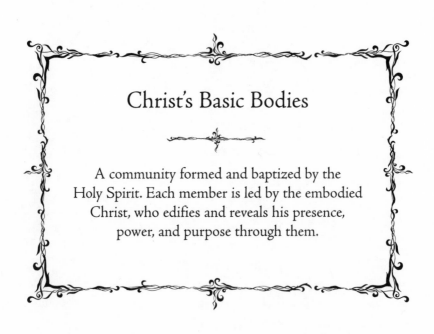

Christ's Basic Bodies

A community formed and baptized by the
Holy Spirit. Each member is led by the embodied
Christ, who edifies and reveals his presence,
power, and purpose through them.

The Inseparable Bond

Just as each of us has one body with many members, and these members do not all have the same function, so in Christ we who are many form one body, and each member belongs to all the others. (Romans 12:4, 5)

There is neither Jew nor Greek, slave nor free, male nor female, for you are all one in Christ Jesus. (Galatians 3:28)

For we are God's workmanship, created in Christ Jesus to do good works, which God prepared in advance for us to do. (Ephesians 2:10)

I conducted a funeral for a precious mother who had slipped into heaven unexpectedly. At the viewing, her daughter sought to embrace her body in the casket. Her brother gently drew her away, saying, "Mary, Mother is not there anymore. That's just her body. She doesn't live there anymore. Let's sit together and recall her life; that's more important than embracing the house she used to use."

So it is with Christ's Basic bodies. The authentic body of Christ has life only because he dwells in it. A gathering of Christians who do not gather under his reign are not his community. He is not only the savior of the *individual* body members, he is also the presence and the power indwelling the body members *collectively*. The Holy Spirit carefully selects and baptizes members to become his new residence on earth.[1]

Christ's Basic Bodies have no life apart from the Head. He is *"the fullness . . . who fills everything in every way."*[2] If Christ's bride has any focus other than her Husband, she is not going to experience the intimacy God intended. If small groups become just another church growth program that fails to help people experience the presence and power of Jesus, they will not effectively train followers of Jesus to become disciples that can make disciples.

It is not possible to speak of the community and not speak of Christ. They are one. The community is not an organization; it is an organism. As the body of man is worthless without a human spirit operating it, so the community is worthless if it is in any way disconnected from the Spirit of Christ. Christ's Basic Bodies are what he uses to reveal his presence. Gerald Martin wrote:

> The next question is, how is the presence manifested? It is found in "one another" ministries, the operation of manifested gifts. I have been sharing a message with our churches on the anointing. I emphasize that Jesus was able to minister in power because of the anointing of the Spirit, referred to in Luke 4:18-19. The key to the anointing was his commitment to the cause for which he came to earth and his compassion for the people for whom he came. Commitment connects us to the power source. Compassion connects us to the needs around us. The body of Christ becomes the conduit. But life only flows when the conduit is connected at both ends.[3]

As long as Christ dwelled in the body of Jesus, he was restricted in the work he could do. That is the reason the resurrected Jesus ascended to be exalted to the throne, to become seated at the right hand of the Father.[4] From that position, God would make him the Head of a new body, one that could penetrate every culture throughout history. All things were put in subjection to him.[5] Moreover, he seated his new body with him in heavenly places.[6]

CHRIST COMPLETES HIS FINAL ASSIGNMENT
BY INHABITING HIS NEW HOUSEHOLD

Ephesians 2:19-22[7] describes Christ as the foundation for a spiritual house. He will dwell within it to redeem the generations. An interesting term, "dwelling place," is used. Christ's incarnation in the body of Jesus would remain for eternity, but he would inhabit a new body to complete his task. The Greek is *katoikētērion*, meaning, "to house permanently." Note the root *oikos* within the word!

Let us further consider this thought from Acts 1:1: "*In my former book, Theophilus, I wrote about all that Jesus began to do and to teach.*" Note that Luke's record of the life of Jesus is to be continued in this new record. The book of Acts would describe what Christ Jesus would *continue* to do as he inhabited his new body. He enlarged the place where his Spirit would dwell. Many bodies will contain his life all over the earth, in every century, in every culture. There is a "new man" described in Colossians 3:10, 11: "*. . . and have put on the new man who is [being] renewed in knowledge, according to the image of Him who created him, where there is neither Greek nor Jew, circumcised nor uncircumcised, barbarian, Scythian, slave nor free, but Christ is all and in all.*" The new dwelling place, the *ekklesia*, exists for the continuation of Christ's activity among men.

Every person "called out" (*ekklesia*) by the Holy Spirit receives the presence of the risen one. Together, these members are then baptized by the Holy Spirit to form a visible body to be controlled by Christ.[8]

In Colosse, the believers were not understanding the place of Christ in their midst. Legalism, asceticism, even mysticism had dulled the mystery of his presence. Paul wrote in Colossians 2:8-10:

See to it that no one takes you captive through hollow and deceptive philosophy, which depends on human tradition and the basic principles of this world rather than on Christ. For in Christ all the fullness of the Deity lives in bodily form, and you have been given fullness in Christ, who is the head over every power and authority.

While they knew they needed Christ, they were being taught they needed many other things as well. They did not recognize their fullness was completely in him. Paul's theme to these dear believers was repeated over and over: *Christ is all you need!*

Let us now reverse this thinking about what *we* need and consider what *God* requires! The Father commissioned Christ—the Anointed One—to disciple all nations (*ethnos*). The invisible God requires a body with many members that will partner with him. Christ's new habitation *must* be a community. His revelation of a triune God who dwells eternally in community cannot be revealed fully by single persons. Therefore, the new body must be composed of humans linked by the Holy Spirit, a body for Christ. If the community is anything other than the body of Christ, it is not fulfilling its purpose.

The new body's deficiencies and flaws will be restored by Christ's power operating within it. As the brain regulates all body functions, so Christ is to be the regulator of all his body does. If there is a stronghold, a soul tie, a generational curse, a secret sin, an unbelieving spirit, a doubting mind in his body, he will edify[9] and purify through a fellow body member chosen to minister to that person.

Why does edification take place? Is it simply to make believers feel better? No! The repair of a body member occurs so Christ may be fully revealed to observers. In James, we learn that when the elders of the community pray for the sick to be healed, they are to anoint with oil. There is no healing in the oil itself; it symbolically confirms the healed person is "set apart" for the work of ministry. The healing allows the body to fulfill the tasks of Christ, to redeem all men. Sickness impacts the effectiveness of Christ's Basic Body. Therefore, the anointing is not just about the healing of the individual, but also about restoring him so he can be active again as a body member.

When we realize the sacredness of Christ's new body, that it contains the literal presence of Christ on earth, it takes on a whole new dimension of importance. No longer can we see the community as simply a small group. It is a sacred basic building block within Christ's new body! This supernatural body is a community formed by God and not man.

We must keep in mind that while Christ's Basic Bodies are basic Christian community, they are not the *whole* community. Like a nuclear family with aunts, uncles, and cousins, Christ's Basic Bodies are part of an extended community. The church is not comprised of independent groups trying to relate to all the other groups in the world. Within the church there are Christ's Basic Bodies, families of Christ's Basic Bodies, and related families of Christ's Basic Bodies.

In a *spiritual* sense, this community of humans is similar to the physical creation of Adam by the Godhead at the beginning of man's history! When this truth begins to be grasped, a passage like the following from 2 Corinthians takes on an entirely new dimension:

Therefore, from now on, we regard no one according to the flesh. Even though we have known Christ according to the flesh, yet now we know Him thus no longer. Therefore, if anyone is in Christ, he is a new creation; old things have passed away; behold, all things have become new. Now all things are of God, who has reconciled us to Himself through Jesus Christ, and has given us the ministry of reconciliation, that is, that God was in Christ reconciling the world to Himself, not imputing their trespasses to them, and has committed to us the word of reconciliation. Now then, we are ambassadors for Christ, as though God were pleading through us: we implore you on Christ's behalf, be reconciled to God. For He made Him who knew no sin to be sin for us, that we might become the righteousness of God in Him.[10]

Paul refers to our basic Christian community as the body of Christ: *"Do you [plural] not know that your bodies are members of Christ?"*[1] What a powerful comment! We must now ask ourselves, "Shall I take my eyes and my ears that belong to Christ and let them see or hear things that are incompatible with his presence within?" Body life is a relationship where the richness of his presence is continually experienced, where the peripheral people are drawn into a community of love. A chorus of yesteryear said it:

> Turn your eyes upon Jesus,
> Look full in His wonderful face,
> And the things of earth will grow strangely dim,
> In the light of His glory and grace.

There is no human replacement for the community inhabited by Christ's Spirit. No large group, no parachurch organization, no small group of Christians seeking to fulfill some particular purpose can take the place of a community of believers who know their connecting link is Christ. As they function as one body, they see the corporate activity of sister communities operating in nearby *oikoses*, revealing Christ to others.

This is much more than a house church movement.[11] It is a worldwide corporate link of communities who celebrate their witness in small Christ-filled groups who know the others are focused on the same goal—revealing his indwelling to other segments of society. In all cases, the goal of an authentic community is to so live and be observed that unbelievers will say, "God is really among you!" All the time, they share in the joy of the witness of other Christ's Basic Bodies and the growth they are experiencing. A network of Christ's Basic Bodies manifests the common presence of Christ.

Thinking in terms of natural family relationships, each family doesn't operate independently. It is part of an extended family. God builds Christ's Basic Bodies revelationally, relationally, and generationally.

Building generationally is much more than creating an institution and handing it down to a son. Becoming spiritual fathers involves raising spiritual sons who will become spiritual fathers raising spiritual sons. That must become part of our DNA.

To make my point, I usually begin all public presentations by saying, "The Christ who dwells in me greets the Christ who dwells in you!" A confused response comes from people who have no awareness that Christ lives in them. How powerful it is when scores of groups proclaim to sister communities, "The Christ who dwells in us greets the Christ who dwells in you!"

Our greatest understanding of the corporate community is to see that it is composed of tens of thousands of groups that are basic communities, and that through such households, Christ works in small segments of the world's society. There is one Lord. There is one life. There is one mission. There is one Redeemer. There is one body. That body is composed of all the households on the face of the earth. There is one rejoicing over the expansion of the kingdom in the hearts of men everywhere.

The community of the Godhead calls for the community of his body on the earth. In its most basic form it is a handful of Spirit-baptized people who live as his family among sister households in the community. Their witness is their presence, observable by all who are nearby. Their lifestyle is one of family life:

> For this reason I bow my knees to the Father of our Lord Jesus Christ, from whom the whole family in heaven and earth is named, that He would grant you, according to the riches of His glory, to be strengthened with might through His Spirit in the inner man, that Christ may dwell in your hearts through faith; that you, being rooted and grounded in love, may be able to comprehend with all the saints what is the width and length and depth and height — to know the love of Christ which passes knowledge; that you may be filled with all the fullness of God.[13]

We are a community in which Christ lives. We are a kingdom of God society whose existence is Christ himself, an organism growing into the fullness of Christ. As Paul so often emphasized, Christ is all, and in all.[14]

IS EACH CHRIST'S BASIC BODY INCARNATED?

Dr. Mark Saucy asks, "Is the church the extension of the incarnation?"[15] He brilliantly defends his position that it is not. He points out the danger of moving in that direction, which can end with the Catholic teaching that the church is incarnated, containing the power to remit sins. He defines this as an ecclesiology that is "too high," even as he accuses evangelicals as having an ecclesiology that is "too low."[16] George Ladd agrees with Saucy, stating:

> It is too much to say that Paul thought of the church as an extension of the incarnation—that just as God was in Christ, Christ is incarnate in the church. Paul preserves a clear distinction between Christ and his church.
>
> The reason Paul draws upon the metaphor of the church as the body of Christ in Romans and Corinthians is . . . to establish the proper relationship of Christians to each other. There is one body but it has many members, and these members differ greatly from one another.[17]

A crystal clear understanding of the relationship is to grasp that not only is Christ in the *ekklesia*, but also that the *ekklesia* is in Christ. Ephesians 4:15 explains the body *"may grow up in all things into Him who is the head–Christ–from whom the whole body, joined and knit together by what every joint supplies, according to the effective working by which every part does its share, causes growth of the body for the edifying of itself in love"* (NKJV).

Christ's Basic Bodies are completely dependent upon Christ for their life and growth. Each one must focus on communion with him as the reason for their existence. Growth does not come from human interaction, but rather from Christ empowering each member to receive his power to edify one another. Thus, the Head is continually operating through the body members to empower them to build up one another. When they gather, this should be their primary task.

Confession of sin or a need is the agenda for each Christ's Basic Body. For example, when the cell groups of the *Eglise Protestante Baptiste Oeuvres et Mission* assemble, each person writes a brief report of a spiritual need in his or her life. This report is then passed to the person to the right, who reads it aloud to the group. Once the burdens and sins have been revealed, the members pray and listen to the voice of Christ giving them spiritual empowerment to deal with the issues present. Edification begins immediately.

The body of Christ must begin its edification processes by the body members revealing the need for Christ's empowerment. As the gathering continues, there is awareness that Christ's Spirit directs the body members who will be used for edification.

The witness of the community, observed by unbelievers present, will then reveal Christ's presence as he empowers *every member*. This will cause unbelievers to cry out, "*God is truly* [in] *you!*"[18] The presence of Christ is manifested when the spiritual gifts operate through compassion to meet people's needs.

Practical Issues

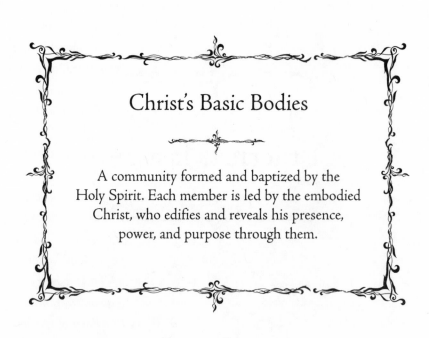

Christ's Basic Bodies

A community formed and baptized by the
Holy Spirit. Each member is led by the embodied
Christ, who edifies and reveals his presence,
power, and purpose through them.

The Kingdom of God and Christ's Basic Bodies

But seek his kingdom, and these things will be given to you as well. Do not be afraid, little flock, for your Father has been pleased to give you the kingdom. Sell your possessions and give to the poor. Provide purses for yourselves that will not wear out, a treasure in heaven that will not be exhausted, where no thief comes near and no moth destroys. For where your treasure is, there your heart will be also. (Luke 12:31-34)

I pray also that the eyes of your heart may be enlightened in order that you may know the hope to which he has called you, the riches of his glorious inheritance in the saints, and his incomparably great power for us who believe. That power is like the working of his mighty strength, which he exerted in Christ when he raised him from the dead and seated him at his right hand in the heavenly realms, far above all rule and authority, power and dominion, and every title that can be given, not only in the present age but also in the one to come. And God placed all things under his feet and appointed him to be head over everything for the church, which is his body, the fullness of him who fills everything in every way. (Ephesians 1:18-23)

For he has rescued us from the dominion of darkness and brought us into the kingdom of the Son he loves, in whom we have redemption, the forgiveness of sins. (Colossians 1:13, 14)

The *kingdom of God* is one of the most remarkable terms of all time. It appeared very near the beginning of history when revealed to Daniel:

In the time of those kings, the God of heaven will set up a kingdom that will never be destroyed, nor will it be left to another people. It will crush all those kingdoms and bring them to an end, but it will itself endure forever.[1]

The understanding of this kingdom is misunderstood in our generation, along with the misconception of "church." It is impossible to repair our understanding of one while ignoring the other. Both must be properly understood if an authentic body of Christ is to appear.

In his definitive book, *The Gospel of the Kingdom*, George Eldon Ladd has provided a brilliant teaching about this subject. There is no better way to understand this topic than to follow his explanations.[2] (In addition, E. Stanley Jones' *The Unshakable Kingdom and the Unchanging Person* is life changing! Add these to your "must read" list!)

The general meaning of *Kingdom*

The term *kingdom* in Greek is *basileia*, meaning "reign" or "rule." We normally think of a kingdom as a geographical area, for instance, the kingdom of England. Thus, we refer to that king ruling over an area of land. It is distinctively a culture separated from its neighbors. "Since 1672, Britannia has been anthropomorphized into a woman wearing a helmet, and carrying a shield and trident. It is a symbol that blends the concepts of empire, militarism and economics."[3]

According to Matthew 4:8, all the kingdoms of this world have been crafted by Satan, each forming cultures offering human pride for its citizens. Thus, this song is sung by British subjects: "*Rule, Britannia, Britannia rule the waves; Britons never will be slaves.*"[4] Note the focus of the kingdom: "empire, militarism and economics." The pride of the kingdom is that they "never will be slaves." However, they did not hesitate to ignore slavery in other cultures. Each kingdom of man is self-serving.

All the cultures of this world are filled with satanically created diversions to blind that people group to the lordship of the true God.

Among the Chinese, the burial custom of placing the cadaver in a box painted to look like a bar of gold reveals their core value of accumulating wealth. In Amsterdam, citizens show their fine furniture through large glass windows of their homes, revealing their core value of possessions. In nearby Paris, the populace boasts that the purity of their language and culture is their most prized treasure.

GOD'S UNSHAKABLE KINGDOM IS UNIQUE

The kingdom of God enters this setting as Christ incarnates Jesus. For the first time in history, a supernatural kingdom appears that ignores all geographical boundaries: "The Lord has established his throne in heaven, and his kingdom rules over all."[5] The intention of the Godhead in creating all things was to reveal his invisible attributes through what was formed. Thus, the psalmist wrote,

All you have made will praise you, O Lord; your saints will extol you. They will tell of the glory of your kingdom and speak of your might, so that all men may know of your mighty acts and the glorious splendor of your kingdom. Your kingdom is an everlasting kingdom, and your dominion endures through all generations.[6]

The kingdom of God is his rule, his reign, over all he has created. John the Baptist announced it: "Repent, for the kingdom of heaven is near."[7] Jesus introduced that reign as the major theme of all he taught and demonstrated its supernatural presence by miracles.

He further instructed his disciples to declare the presence of the kingdom using both words and supernatural deeds. The announcement by them was to be accompanied by healing the sick and raising the dead—signs of the kingdom presence: "*Heal the sick who are there and tell them, 'The kingdom of God is near you.'* "[8]

By examining all Jesus taught about the kingdom as recorded in the four gospels, it is obvious that this was his supreme message. We might say with reverence that he was obsessed with this theme and spoke of it both in plain words and in many parables. He described it as a "mystery" (something hidden from view)[9] he would reveal to them.

The reign of God in this age was declared and demonstrated by his power and presence. In Mark 10:15, Jesus said we must "receive the kingdom of God" as little children. What is to be received takes place when we totally surrender ourselves to his rule. Paul and James described the intensity of this surrender by referring to themselves as "slaves" of God.[10] Ladd writes,

> What is received? The Church? Heaven? What is received is God's rule. In order to enter the future realm of the Kingdom, one must submit himself in perfect trust to God's rule here and now. . . . we are to seek God's righteousness—His sway, His rule, His reign in our lives.
>
> When we pray, "Thy kingdom come," are we praying for heaven to come to earth? In a sense we are praying for this; but . . . . apart from the reign of God, heaven is meaningless. Therefore, what we pray for is, "Thy kingdom come; *thy will be done* on earth as it is in heaven."[11]

CHRIST'S BASIC BODIES REVEAL THE PRESENCE OF THE KINGDOM

In the same way that the body of Jesus—incarnated by Christ— manifested the lifestyle and the power of the kingdom (*basileia*), even so his presence in his Basic Bodies today should manifest its presence and power. The location of the kingdom of God in this present age is first of all in each "called-out one" and then formally in his holy body, the people who are baptized together to become his habitation.

The kingdom may be studied, it may be evaluated, and it may be made an idol to be worshipped with tithes and offerings. But it is never authentic until it is the life force that is evidenced by Christ's presence and power. It is shocking to see how we tiptoe around this issue! The lack of power and demonstration of his presence in churchianity is obvious, first of all, to those unreached by our invitations to follow Christ.

It must be considered *mandatory* for an authentic Christ's Basic Body to manifest the signs and wonders of kingdom life. When the Spirit of the Lord is upon it, it will impact the poor, the captives, the blind, and the bruised. Its ministry will be a divine flow from within through the group, causing unbelievers to fall on their faces and cry out, "God is among you!"

Because we sheepishly admit we are not capable of such a lifestyle, we excuse ourselves by explaining that such activities were only for the first century, that today's "miracles" may not be so dramatic, or by flatly creating a theology that relegates such "excesses" to the fringe groups. Or, we seek to make a show in public arenas that at least *some* among us have special supernatural abilities, and we sit in wonder as they show us what we cannot do that they have received a special anointing not available to all of us.

Are Christ's Basic Bodies the kingdom?

It would be better to ask, "Are they a *part* of the kingdom?" They are within it to preach it and proclaim it. The kingdom exists wherever the body of Christ exists, but it is far more. The song of the twenty-four elders in Revelation 5:9, 10 identified all of the redeemed as a kingdom because they share in Christ's rule:

You are worthy to take the scroll and to open its seals, because you were slain, and with your blood you purchased men for God from every tribe and language and people and nation. You have made them to be a kingdom and priests to serve our God, and they will reign on the earth.

Ladd comments, "The Kingdom of God in this verse is not the realm of God's reign; it is God's reign itself, a reign which is shared with those who surrender themselves to it."[12]

CHRIST'S BASIC BODIES MUST FOCUS ON PRAYER

Consider the account of Jesus' disciples who came back from an assignment sharing excitedly about the manifestations they had experienced.[13] Then a negative report came from a father whose son endured seizures. Jesus was indignant and said to his disciples, *"How long shall I put up with you?"*[14] After he healed the boy, the embarrassed disciples asked, *"Why couldn't we drive it out?"* His response should be carefully considered: *"This kind can come out only by prayer."*[15]

Kingdom living cannot exist unless there is a clear communication established between Christ and his body members. A missing ingredient is a priority on prayer. A direct link between powerlessness and prayerlessness can be made. The King of the kingdom prayed all night while the disciples slept. The King could heal; the disciples could not.

A focus on authentic prayer must mark the emergence of Christ's bodies all over the world. Thousands of illustrations can be found in the history of the church about the power of prayer, but few are forthcoming from this generation in the Western world. Meanwhile, the underground church in China grows because of its prayer life.

Under Japanese persecution in the middle of the last century, the Korean church became a praying community, packing out their unheated buildings at 5:30 a.m. to cry out to God for deliverance. The world was impressed by the reports of their prayer life and the answers that came. As the years passed and the nation became prosperous, the passion turned into tradition. When I visit Korean churches today, I often find the pastor has a bed in his office to sleep overnight, but the attendance for morning prayer has dwindled to a faithful few. I have attended some of those meetings and saw for myself that the buildings are no longer crowded. Yet the reality of prayer is experienced by many of their leaders. In Houston, a strong Korean cell-based church has a pastor who remains undisturbed in his office from 5 to 8:30 A.M. every morning. His prayer life is obvious in teaching the body members what priorities they should have in praying constantly.

Where prayer is emphasized, the presence and power of Christ are manifested, not only among the Chinese house churches but also in persecution-ridden nations like Indonesia. In the church in South Africa I mentioned in an earlier chapter, the leadership provides a three-year training for believers who are then commissioned to plant new churches. Their first preparation focuses on their prayer life. They meet regularly for prayer; on Saturday mornings I have watched them march in a circle, interceding and searching for God's guidance. When I asked how they initiated walking and praying together, Harold Weitz explained that because the prayer meetings lasted so long, physical activity stimulated their bodies to remain alert.

A survey taken among American pastors by Touch Outreach Ministries some time ago reported that the typical length of time each one prayed was *seven minutes a day*. As R. G. Lee used to ask, "If the gold rusts, what will the iron do?" The kingdom of God is built from intimate communication between Christ and his body. This must be a primary focus if we are to exhibit the presence and power of Christ.

The proof is in *authentic* manifestations

I have never backed away from insisting the supernatural events of the kingdom take place today. Ruth and I have experienced a blind girl receiving her sight and a woman with cataracts healed. Prayer for barren wombs has produced babies. A baby deaf from birth was healed in Abidjan the same night a demonized woman received her sanity after living naked for months in a wooded area. I staunchly believe the kingdom is being revealed in many parts of the world right now.

I have also received rebuke for being "too strict" for discouraging fake manifestations so common in the American church today. I have been told to "let the wheat and the tares grow together." The problem with this compromise is that those who "fake it" think that's what all the others are doing. Is there any ethical principle that endorses "fake it until you make it"? Manifesting the presence and the power of God is not a skill to be developed by practice. It is not man's doing, but God's energizing. Because there is 100 percent reality *every* time God works, the authentic draws unbelievers. Why settle for contrived experiences to "look spiritual" to each other? Is not a kingdom lifestyle a rebuke on everything false and to rejoice in the reality that is present? Men cannot build the kingdom. It is a miracle. It is the act of God. It is the supernatural. It is *God's* reign! Ladd points out this threefold fact:

> *First,* some passages refer to the Kingdom of God as God's reign. *Second,* some passages refer to God's Kingdom as the realm into which we may now enter to experience the blessing of His reign; *Third,* still other passages refer to a future realm, which will come only with the return of our Lord Jesus Christ, into which we shall then enter and experience the fullness of His reign.
>
> God's reign expresses itself in different stages through redemptive history. Therefore, men may enter into the realm of God's reign in its several stages of manifestation and experience the blessings of His reign in differing degrees.[16]

In the present stage, the kingdom is within us. In the future stage, all other kingdoms will be abolished and Christ alone will reign over all the earth. All of history is in the control of the Godhead. Before the foundations of the earth were laid, he composed it in linear progressions. His first and last notes are consonant with the harmonic unit to which the progression prolongs. We are in the midst of that history and participate in his plan only when we surrender our own plans. In Jesus, Christ introduced the kingdom of God. Its presence exists today on the earth as his reign in the lives of "called out" persons. We are created so he will be revealed through us.

Scriptures describing the kingdom

Here is a summary of Scripture relating to these passages:

+ Christ's Basic Bodies will penetrate every part of history and geography in this present age so the indwelling Christ can share his presence, his message, and his reign (Revelation 5:9, 10).

+ Every believer is called out by the Father. Man must respond to that call to receive citizenship in the kingdom (John 6:44).

+ Every believer is immediately removed from a self-directed life. The first official act of the Holy Spirit upon sealing that life is to submerge the person as a member of Christ's Basic Bodies. In the context of this community further sanctification will take place (Philippians 2:12). *There are no independent, unattached Christians in the kingdom of God!* (Romans 6:3; 1 Corinthians 12:13).

+ Every experience in the life of Christ's body members is "boot camp" training for the coming age. The short period of time we live in this world provides us with opportunity to receive and live out core values that are preparing us for future kingdom assignments (Matt. 25:14-24).

+ At the end of this age, Jesus Christ will appear in bodily form to establish the overthrow of the present order. At that time we will all appear at the Bema judgment to be evaluated for potential assignments in the age to come (1 Corinthians 3:10-16).

+ The coming age will begin by the dissolving of all the cultures of this world (Revelation 11:15).

+ Satan will be cast into a bottomless pit to remove his evil influence from the environment (Revelation 20:2, 3).

+ The kingdom, or reign, will be established by Christ. Those who are chosen at the Bema judgment will govern in this one world government (2 Tim. 2:11-13).

+ For one thousand years this society will prove that a perfect environment will not produce perfect humans, that their rebellion against God's reign over them is inherent within their nature (2 Peter 3:10-17).

+ At the end of the thousand years there will be an attempted rebellion. Satan will be temporarily released from the bottomless pit (Revelation 11:7). This uprising will be quenched by Christ (Revelation 20:7-10).

+ Human death will, for the first time, be abolished forever (Revelation 21:4).

+ The Great White Throne judgment will bring final sentence to all whose names are not found in the Lamb's Book of Life (Revelation 20:11-15).

+ Heaven and earth will be completely renovated. The *Shekinah* fire will consume all the possessions and creations made by mankind (2 Peter 3:7-12).

+ A reconstruction will take place with Jerusalem, the Holy City, becoming a cube of massive size (Revelation 21:2-5).

+ Having completed all his tasks assigned by the Godhead, Christ will surrender all he has completed to the Father. Eternity will continue ... and there will be no more time (1 Corinthians 15:24-28).

THE AWESOME PURPOSE OF THESE SHORT YEARS IN WHICH WE LIVE

Beginning with his incarnation in Jesus, Christ has been fulfilling his assignments so the kingdom will reach its final consummation. The events of this present time are preparing for the next era, when Christ will end the kingdoms of this earth and establish his reign over the earth. It will begin with his return to earth. Note the events that involve us: if we have already died, we will be taken from graves to meet him. If we are living, we will be caught up to meet him in the air.[17]

In the same way an army trains its troops to know how to live and function when war breaks out, so Christ is preparing Basic Bodies for the future events when he establishes the kingdom of God and reigns over it. As the president of the United States appoints cabinet members and judges when taking office, so Christ will fill the global positions necessary to manage his kingdom.

Reflect again on the parables that discuss the present and the future aspects of the kingdom. The pearl of great price parable illustrates our selecting the kingdom as more important than all our accumulated possessions. The lost coin parable helps us see the importance of not losing our valued place in the kingdom. Jesus' parables are all focused on the loyal citizens of the kingdom in this age. We should meditate often on them.

In addition, Jesus described the uniqueness of kingdom living when he presented the Sermon on the Mount and the Beatitudes. As Ladd points out, "The righteousness of the Kingdom of God demands an attitude of heart which is not motivated by selfish concerns, which does not demand even one's legitimate rights."[18]

As the clock ticks, the record of our values and actions is being carefully evaluated. These details will influence our standing in the future kingdom. Those who are faithful over much in this life, who produce gold, silver, and precious stones instead of wood, hay, and straw, will be appointed accordingly to ministerial positions in the kingdom.

Straight ahead lies one thousand years for Christ to prepare the kingdom. What we focus on now will determine what we will do during that millennium. But there seems to be even more to consider when we think of how we are living today: at the conclusion of the thousand years, Christ will turn his completed kingdom over to the Father and time will be no more! What will that transfer of ownership involve? *A fully developed kingdom structure, with all governing structures intact.* We are indeed conjecturing—for little is written about this eternal kingdom when God himself will assume ownership—but we will surely be positioned in its eternal government! Should that not cause us to ponder deeply what our values are for living today?

For most, the brief years on this earth are less than one hundred. This is our "boot camp" period. Then a thousand years of service will follow. The foolish activities and interests of this age will not be replicated in the coming kingdom. Purity and righteousness will be the norm. Christians in this age who focus on carnal activities will be quite uncomfortable there. Holiness is a most uncomfortable environment for the unholy:

> *We must pay careful attention, therefore, to what we have heard, so that we do not drift away. For if the message spoken by angels was binding, and every violation and disobedience received its just punishment, how shall we escape if we ignore such a great salvation? This salvation, which was first announced by the Lord, was confirmed to us by those who heard him. God also testified to it by signs, wonders and various miracles, and gifts of the Holy Spirit distributed according to his will.*[19]

The kingdom makes one demand of each person: decide, once and for all time, that I am under God's reign. "Repentance" means to make a total about-face from a self-controlled life to a surrendered will. It causes us to pray, "Lord Christ, I choose *your* will in the place of *my* will from this moment on, concerning every decision I make." Or, to put it in the shorter words of Jesus, *"Thy kingdom come. Thy will be done on earth as it is in heaven."*

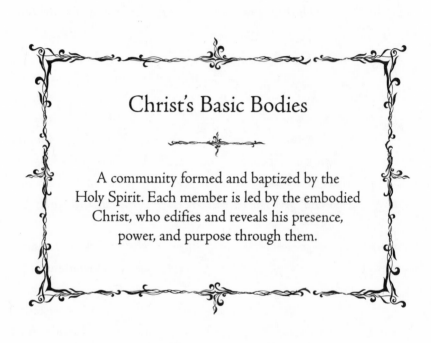

Christ's Basic Bodies

A community formed and baptized by the
Holy Spirit. Each member is led by the embodied
Christ, who edifies and reveals his presence,
power, and purpose through them.

How Are Christ's Basic Bodies Formed?

Unless the Lord builds the house, its builders labor in vain. Unless the Lord watches over the city, the watchmen stand guard in vain.　　(Psalms 127:1)

Jesus asked, "Who do you say I am?" Simon Peter answered, "You are the Christ, the Son of the living God."Jesus replied, "Blessed are you, Simon son of Jonah, for this was not revealed to you by man, but by my Father in heaven. And I tell you that . . . on this rock I will build my church, and the gates of Hades will not overcome it I will give you the keys of the kingdom of heaven; whatever you bind on earth will be bound in heaven, and whatever you loose on earth will be loosed in heaven." (Matthew 16:15-19)

For all of you who were baptized into Christ have clothed yourselves with Christ.　　　　　　　　　　　　　　　　(Galatians 3:27)

Over the past forty-one years, Ruth and I have consistently participated in weekly cell groups. Most were truly God-made. As I reflect about them, there are distinct characteristics that are the same in all of them, described in 1 John 2:12-14. With few exceptions, the Holy Spirit places together spiritual little children, young men, and fathers. Thus, the maturity of the body members allows them to serve each other and observe growth together:

> *I write to you, dear children,*
> > *because your sins have been forgiven on account of his name.*
> *I write to you, fathers,*
> > *because you have known him who is from the beginning.*

I write to you, young men,
   because you have overcome the evil one.
I write to you, dear children,
   because you have known the Father.
I write to you, fathers,
   because you have known him who is from the beginning.
I write to you, young men,
   because you are strong,
   and the word of God lives in you,
   and you have overcome the evil one (emphasis mine).

Ruth and I were "fathers" who joined Cal and Shirley, members of our body who were spiritually "young men." They had a love for Christ and sensitivity for the unreached. Shirley met a Jewish woman at work whose marriage and family were in turmoil. Carefully cultivating her, she led our group to pray almost daily over the drama in that hurting family. After Cal and Shirley quietly financed a week at a Christian retreat center for the wife, she became aware of the selfless spirit in her new friend. Next came visits to our group, after the husband said, "We are Jews, but we are really impressed by your faith. We would like you to explain it all to us." Cal offhandedly said, "Well, you know, you live just five doors down from a man who knows all there is to know about the Jewish carpenter!"

This began their addition to our group as we spent Sunday afternoon in my living room discussing Isaiah and their Messiah. After about five weeks, I asked the husband this question: "Knowing all you have learned about Jesus Christ, are you able to turn on your heel and leave him behind you?" (He told me later the question was like a punch in the jaw.)

He turned to his wife and asked, "What would you say to that question?" With mascara-drenched tears dripping down her cheeks, she said, "I have not known how to tell you this, but two weeks ago after we met here I went into our bedroom closet, closed the door, and invited him to live in my life." He paused only for a moment and then said, "I cannot walk away. What do I do?" Cal stood up and suggested we join hands in a circle. The man gave his life to Christ as we witnessed his words of confession.

The Holy Spirit had just added the "little children" to our group. We began to grow together, adding other couples until we were too large to have true community. At multiplication time, we had experienced several growth experiences as births and new "young men" developed to help them.

It is possible for Christ's *ekklesia* to be so properly aligned with heaven that the Spirit of Christ actually displaces the powers of darkness. To the degree that the *ekklesia* is joined to Christ and Christ alone, his presence guards that body. That sacred dwelling place for Christ is destined to reveal him to all men in all generations, and the gates of hell cannot stop it!

THE FORMATION OF CHRIST'S BASIC BODIES

Step one: Individual selection by the Holy Spirit

"Now you are the body of Christ, and each one of you is a part of it."[1] The body is composed of selected persons. The Holy Spirit calls God-rejecters to enter a community. Those who respond to his call are immediately sealed by him (Ephesians 4:30) and receive the presence of Christ, who dwells in them:

I have been crucified with Christ and I no longer live, but Christ lives in me. The life I live in the body, I live by faith in the Son of God, who loved me and gave himself for me.[2]

This entrance takes place the moment we are redeemed from self-ownership through Christ's sacrifice on the cross. This event is called the *gospel,* or the *good news.* It is far more than just a *message.* Conversion is an awesome experience as one is invaded by the very presence of Christ, not just an acknowledgement of his existence. Jesus described it as a supernatural birth in John 3:3, an event that allows blind eyes to see the kingdom reign of God.

There is no greater "good news" than that Christ has cleansed us by his sacrificial *death* so he might inhabit us with his *life*. It is his indwelling life that is the source of healing, deliverance, and God's favor. When we understand this, we see salvation's message from God's perspective, not man's! *This* is the true gospel: "Christ in me!"

When Paul wrote in Romans that he was not ashamed of the gospel, he was not referring to God having just a "wonderful plan for our lives." The good news is this: "Now you are the body of Christ!" The purpose of redemption is to produce body parts. That selection always includes being baptized into Christ's Basic Bodies:

> *The body is a unit, though it is made up of many parts; and though all its parts are many, they form one body. So it is with Christ. For we were all baptized by one Spirit into one body—whether Jews or Greeks, slave or free—and we were all given the one Spirit to drink.*[3]

Not for even one second is there a time for a self-governing Christian to exist. It's all one process: we are called out, we are sealed by the Spirit, Christ enters us, we are joined to other body members, and we storm the gates of hell! N. T. Wright comments,

> Paul was concerned to build up the church as the reworked chosen people of God. . . . Those who were called by God when the gospel was preached were to become a single community, meeting together for worship and prayer, and not least helping one another practically, which would normally include financial support. . . . A new community has sprung up in which people from all kinds of backgrounds, with no natural affinity of kin or shared business, are welcoming one another and supporting one

another practically. If that isn't God's power at work, Paul indicates, he doesn't know what is.[4]

Christ is the center of it all

We exist for him to fulfill his plan through us. His plan is that all who are called out should be immediately inhabited by his presence and power. The *ekklesia* exists solely for Christ; Christ is the sole focus for the *ekklesia*.

When an organized church does not understand this, it forms an organization, not the *ekklesia*. There is a heaven-and-earth difference between God-made Christ's Basic Bodies and man-made church structures. Christ's Basic Bodies are the basic communities of God. They cluster to create the greater body of Christ.

This is what we have misunderstood: the greater body does not come first. (Does a house form the bricks used to build it?) Each called-out person is destined to be baptized into a biblical community. It is the first official act of the Holy Spirit in the life of new believers.

Look at all the hands and arms and inward parts that float unattached today! We have offered a no-connection gospel message and we have spawned unconnected Christians by the millions. They can exist alone with nothing more than a book or a radio or a television program. They have no concept of body life and their distant media "teachers" know that, should they ever understand true body life, their independent financial support base would disintegrate. It's a "catch 22" situation. The more the electronic gospel goes forth, the greater the problem becomes. Most serious is what it does in other continents.

Imagine a poor man in a wooden shack watching the American Christians in an opulent setting sharing how God has blessed them with prosperity. In faraway Nairobi, a report comes about a pastor who drives an expensive car and lives in a mansion while his church members live in shacks. When confronted about his lifestyle, he says it is because he wants to show others how God will bless the faithful with riches. Ugh!

Step two: Communion with Christ

In Ephesians 3:7-12, Paul shares the intention of God in shaping the *ekklesia* to be Christ's body. He had a special destiny for this special community and it had to do with the "rulers and authorities in the heavenly realms":

> *I became a servant . . . to make plain to everyone the administration*
> *of this mystery, which for ages past was kept hidden in God, who*
> *created all things. His intent was that now, through the church, the*
> *manifold wisdom of God should be made known to the rulers and*
> *authorities in the heavenly realms, according to his eternal purpose*
> *which he accomplished in Christ Jesus our Lord. In him and through*
> *faith in him we may approach God with freedom and confidence.*

Therefore, the *formation*, *activity*, and *witness* of the *ekklesia* are influenced by being baptized into the body of Christ:

The *formation* of Christ's Basic Bodies is the work of the Holy Spirit, not the apostles. The contemporary term "church planter" defines a person forming a religious structure, which may or may not develop "called-out people." If the planter is doing so from a desire for personal significance, the thumbprint of that person will shape the community.

The *activity* of Christ's Basic Bodies is directed by Christ. He is quite capable of sending his presence where it is needed. After all, he is the Lord of the harvest! When he directs the body members, they will be sent to the whitened harvest. In advance, the Holy Spirit has been active among the God-rejecters, calling out to all, some of whom are ready to receive. The book of Acts is filled with reports of those guided to confront responsive persons. There are daily additions to God's family, and he knows where the crop is ripe for reaping.

The *witness* of Christ's bodies reveals Christ's inner presence. The members of his body must maintain an intimate and consistent communion with Christ. They must be able to hear his voice, sense his guidance, think his thoughts, and execute his activities. The Holy Spirit fully participates:

In the same way, the Spirit helps us in our weakness. We do not know what we ought to pray for, but the Spirit himself intercedes for us with groans that words cannot express. And he who searches our hearts knows the mind of the Spirit, because the Spirit intercedes for the saints in accordance with God's will.[5]

As the Spirit intercedes for us as we commune with the indwelling Christ, even so Christ himself *"is at the right hand of God and is also interceding for us."*[6]

This is not "commonplace Christianity!" Seldom are the people of God taught how to hear the voice of the Son of God indwelling them. Most of the time they are hearing the voices of human leaders giving instructions or their own inner voice. Human projects, human agendas, human meetings overwhelm today's believers. Little is really God-directed. What we must strive for is to secure freedom for Christ's Basic Bodies from man's control.

Step three: The movement of Christ in his Basic Body

In the illustration on the following page, the various actions that take place between Christ and his basic body are described.

Begin by viewing the circle in the upper left. The administrator of Christ's Basic Bodies is Christ. The body has an *inward* fellowship with him through prayer. They have fellowship with one another as a *community* led by him. They *celebrate* his presence by their worship. They receive *revelation* from him to direct their ministries. They *edify* one another as he flows his gifts into them to build up one another. He directs their paths to reach into the unreached as they *witness* of his inner presence. (At this stage they are *observed* as a body by unbelievers.) The fruit of the conversions causes the natural

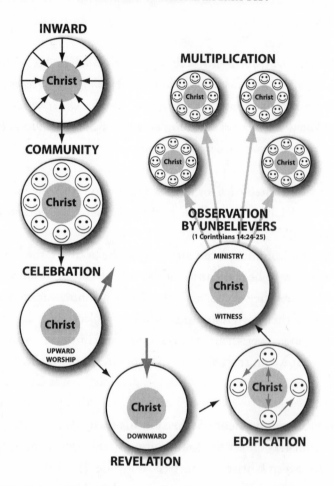

THE MOVEMENT OF CHRIST IN HIS BASIC BODY

multiplication of Christ's Basic Bodies to begin.

Perhaps the Chinese house churches come closest to a model in our generation to guide us. Cut off from many of the radio and television stations that flood the ears of Christians in the Western world, they focus on the pure life and words of the one who indwells them. It is crucial for us to do the same.

It's all about Christ directing the life of his body. Many cannot adjust to what would happen to their ministries if rigid controls were dropped from church life. Nevertheless, Christ's Basic Bodies will flourish most in streamlined, permission-giving communities.

THE ROLE OF THE EQUIPPERS
IN CHRIST'S BASIC BODY

Much work is to be done by kingdom servants who equip the body members. There is plenty of room for the apostles, prophets, evangelists, pastors, and teachers *in supportive roles.*]Ephesians 4:11-13 states:

> It was he [Christ] *who gave some to be apostles, some to be prophets, some to be evangelists, and some to be pastors and teachers, to prepare God's people for works of service, so that the body of Christ may be built up until we all reach unity in the faith and in the knowledge of the Son of God and become mature, attaining to the whole measure of the fullness of Christ.*

These are *bottom* positions, not *top* ranks. These are not offices, meant to dress up men with titles but rather to perform tasks. Like John the Baptist, those who are so empowered by Christ should say, "He must increase; I must decrease." Effective activities by these five equippers will expand the life of the body members without interfering with their direct link to Christ as the Head.

A classic example of the contemporary fear of men losing status and control within organized religion is seen in this scathing reaction by an editor of a prominent Christian magazine, in his review of *Revolution*[7] by George Barna:

> Says Barna: "The Bible neither describes nor promotes the local church as we know it today." . . . If you still go to church, Barna makes you to feel like a weirdo. We are behind the times. According to Barna's research, the really relevant Christians

who care about Jesus and love people will say adios to their pastors and write Ichabod on the doors of ecclesiastical buildings. He envisions a "spiritual awakening" in which people are drawn away from the church, not drawn toward it. Barna even provides a creed we can recite at the end of the book, which includes this statement: "I am not called to attend or join a church. I am called to be the Church."

The editor completely missed Barna's point. People who are led by other people are insulated by at least one layer from the Master's voice. That is one of the reasons why the church is dying. There is a desperate cry in our world for Christ-directed ministries, not man-directed projects.

Ministry so executed will be radically different from what we now experience! This Christ-directed lifestyle was experienced in the early church. Without structures and *with* Christ-given creativity, early believers lit fires that finally burned down the Roman Empire. Some who were burned alive in those fires did so singing praises. What Christ gave them to live for was worth dying for. (Church programs have yet to produce a rejoicing martyr!)

Why should we consider it radical for the body of Christ to be directed by him? *"In all your ways acknowledge him"* is a shibboleth that has been made into wall plaques but seldom obeyed.[8] Jesus' suggestion to *"seek first his kingdom"* in Matthew 6:33 is another shibboleth to most Christians. Yet, it promises that if we have no second source of supply, all we need will be provided by the Father.

There is such a variance between what we claim to believe and how we live out those beliefs. It is time for us to understand that the authentic body of Christ must hear his voice and follow his directions. *Where do we experience that in today's churchianity?*

If every one of Christ's Basic Bodies were to experience true communion with his indwelling presence, amazing conversions would take place around the world. The "mission agenda" of each Christ's group must be left to the Head. Peter was guided to Cornelius. Philip was sent to assist a man from Ethiopia. Paul knew exactly where his team should go when a vision directed him to Macedonia. *Can we not expect Christ to lead his bodies to the places he wants to impact?*

In China today, the Back to Jerusalem Movement[9] is successfully challenging hundreds of house church members to relocate. Thousands of Chinese Christians have sold their homes, quit their jobs, and bought one-way tickets to to Islamic cities. They are called by Christ to take the gospel message "back to Jerusalem," which means extending the missionary presence into the restricted Muslim nations. This is a clear example of the sacrifice readily accepted by those who listen to Christ and not organizations promoting movements.

The apostles did not stay long in one spot because they knew Christ would direct his new bodies. Returning a couple of years later, they observed apostles, prophets, evangelists, pastors, and teachers formed by Christ in their absence. Paul specifically states in Ephesians 4:11 that Christ himself provides these equippers for his body. Like cream rising to the top, the servants who will model the mature ministries will spontaneously develop if man does not tinker with controlling structures.

This is exactly what Barna is calling for, and so do many others who have no vested interests to protect in the existing profit-making structures of today's churchianity. Beware you do not grieve the Holy Spirit.

HOW CAN THE EARLY CHURCH GUIDE US TO THE END-TIME CHURCH?

A century ago, Schlatter shared insights about the early church we must implement today:

> The reason for this retention by the apostles of the leadership of the Church was that the Church did not break away from Jesus. She refused to oppose the Spirit and the Christ against each

other, but saw in their joint working the revelation of God. Christian thinking was Trinitarian, i.e., they saw in the working of the Christ and in the working of the Spirit the one revelation of God, not granted to a special elite, but bestowed in its fullness on all. Thus the leaders appointed by Jesus retained their authority. The prophets were not raised above them, but kept their place within the Church, for they became prophets only because they shared in what Christ had gained for all. So the Church was in duty bound to form her own judgement about the prophet's message, -and retained her freedom over against him.[10]

Prophecy is one of the five areas where Christ appointed equippers. In Christ's Basic Bodies, all prophesy, not just some:

Acts 2:17, 18: *In the last days, God says, I will pour out my Spirit on all people. Your sons and daughters will prophesy, your young men will see visions, your old men will dream dreams. Even on my servants, both men and women, I will pour out my Spirit in those days, and they will prophesy.*

1 Corinthians 14:5: *I would rather have you prophesy. He who prophesies is greater than one who speaks in tongues, unless he interprets, so that the church may be edified.*

1 Corinthians 14:31: *For you can all prophesy in turn so that everyone may be instructed and encouraged.*

1 Corinthians 14:39, 40: *Therefore, my brothers, be eager to prophesy, and do not forbid speaking in tongues. But everything should be done in a fitting and orderly way.*

Any time body members share what Christ desires to flow through them, they are sharing in what Christ had gained for all. We shall deal with this in a later chapter, but here it should be established that communion with Christ brought forth his direct guidance for the life and tasks of the body.

The sacredness of Christ's Basic Bodies

As we recall the sacredness of the ark of the covenant, we might also consider the sacredness of Christ's Basic Bodies. Both the ark and the *ekklesia* are containers for the Lord. The ark did not need the support of men. When Uzzah reached out to steady it, the Lord's anger burned against him because of his irreverent act and he died.[11] It is a solemn responsibility to participate in serving the present ark that has been created for Christ to inhabit. What does the Godhead think of the way body members are left unattended while churchianity goes its merry way?

The goal of Christ is to see the called-out ones of this generation prepared to reign with him. Where are the apostles, prophets, evangelists, pastors, and teachers, who are faithfully equipping God's people for the work of ministry? We have raised an illiterate generation of Christians who have busied themselves reading their Bibles, attending endless meetings in buildings and homes, but powerless and visionless.

Judgment day is coming! To whom much has been given, much will be required.

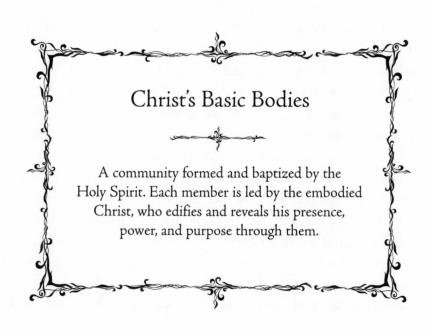

Christs Basic Bodies

A community formed and baptized by the
Holy Spirit. Each member is led by the embodied
Christ, who edifies and reveals his presence,
power, and purpose through them.

The "Energizings"
The Source and the Supplier

But to each one of us grace has been given as Christ apportioned it. This is
why it says: "When he ascended on high, he led captives in his train and gave
gifts to men."   (Ephesians 4:7, 8)

Many years ago, a move of God took place in San Antonio, Texas.
Many showgirls and bouncers were converted out of nightclub
businesses and a powerful stirring among backslidden Christians began.
I was invited to come and participate in the discipling of these new
believers. When I arrived, one of the church staff questioned whether I
had been "filled with the Spirit" in the manner he had recently
experienced. I was his senior both in age and in knowing the hand of
God at work, but he made it clear that unless I had experienced the Holy
Spirit as he had, I would surely quench the move of God in their midst.

Particularly, I was obligated to "demonstrate" the validity of my filling
by exercising the power to heal and drive out demons. This seemed to be
the test applied to judge my spiritual character. It was at that time in my
journey I began to ingest the truth about the "great secret" Paul
described, that Christ dwelling within was our greatest legacy.

As I sought to explain that the "gifts" described in the epistles were
given by Christ and that he was the One sent to be resident in our lives,
my young colleague's filter screened out all I was trying to share. I was
considered to be outside the "experience" everyone else had received.
After all, it was all about the Holy Spirit and only the Holy Spirit! I was
told Christ was secondary to the Spirit in today's world.

THE PLACE OF CHRIST IN EDIFICATION

As discussed in chapter two, doctrinal distortions left over from the last century must be addressed. Many have taught that the Holy Spirit is the source or originator of the gifts. The phrase often used, even for book titles, has referred to "the gifts of the Holy Spirit." While the Holy Spirit is clearly the *transporter* of them to the body members who will manifest them, Christ is the source described in Scripture, as declared in the fourth chapter of Paul's letter to the Ephesians.

In reality, we should be acknowledging "The gifts of Christ." (Study the diagram below.)

Christ and the Holy Spirit's Activity in His Present Body

This illustration shows that Christ is the presence, power, and purpose of the Basic Body. He—not the Holy Spirit—is the source of all spiritual gifts. Christ is specifically mentioned as the one who empowers the apostles, prophets, evangelists, pastors, and teachers.

In the diagram, the Holy Spirit is everywhere as the agent of Christ to the body members. He is the *"one called alongside to help."* The Holy Spirit carries the groans of the body members to Christ. The Holy Spirit then carries the spiritual power of Christ back to the members of the body. As they manifest the spiritual gifts, they know the source of them is Christ and the empowering of them is through the work of the Holy Spirit. Thus, their relationship to Christ is through the Holy Spirit's activity within the body.

In no way does this diminish the activity of the Holy Spirit! Rather, it explains the precious interaction between Christ and the Spirit in the activity of Christ's Basic Bodies. The centrality of Christ—as the ambassador of the Godhead to mankind— is fully assisted by the Holy Spirit's activity.

Ephesians 4:7, 8 refers to Psalm 68:18 and is a restatement of that passage:

> *When you ascended on high,*
> *you led captives in your train;*
> *you received gifts from men,*
> *even from the rebellious —*
> *that you, O Lord God, might dwell there.*

But to each one of us grace has been given as Christ apportioned it. *This is why it says: "When he ascended on high, he led captives in his train and gave gifts to men"* (Ephesians 4:7, 8). Paul's words lead to several important thoughts:

+ The term "each one" (*hekastos*) must be understood as all-inclusive. This word appears in 1 Corinthians 14:24, where "each one" is prophesying. The grace gifts of Christ are for *all* believers, not just some. The distribution is unlimited.

+ The *measure* of Christ's gifts is also unlimited. It is based on the victory of the Resurrected One. By leading captivity captive, he has totally overcome everything that imprisons mankind.

+ Christ gives the unlimited distribution in unlimited measure to all who believe. This passage makes it very clear that the empowerment of God's children to lead captivity captive is given by Christ himself.

Passages in Ephesians 4 further direct our attention to the centrality of Christ and also the role of the Holy Spirit in his new body. In verse 15, Christ is shown to be the Head of the body. In verse 16, Christ empowers *"every part,"* causing growth through edification.

The gifts of Christ are for building up his body. He is clearly the *source* of the gifts in Ephesians 4:15-16:

Instead, speaking the truth in love, we will in all things grow up into him who is the Head, that is, Christ. From him the whole body, joined and held together by every supporting ligament, grows and builds itself up in love, as each part does its work.

In verse 21, the focus is on our learning from Christ: "*You heard of him and were taught in him . . .*" We recall again the words of Jesus explaining the Holy Spirit would teach us about Christ and all he taught.[1]

When we consider the Holy Spirit's role in the body, several verses give us insight into his interaction with us in Christ's Basic Body:

+ In Ephesians 4:30, we see we can *grieve* the Holy Spirit: "*And do not grieve the Holy Spirit of God, with whom you were sealed for the day of redemption.*"
+ In Acts 7:51, we see we can *resist* the Holy Spirit: "*You always resist the Holy Spirit!*"
+ In John 20:22, 23, we see we can *receive* the Holy Spirit: "*And with that he breathed on them and said, 'Receive the Holy Spirit. If you forgive anyone his sins, they are forgiven; if you do not forgive them, they are not forgiven.'*"

To realize the critical role the Holy Spirit has in body life activities is to gain new respect for his servant role. As he approaches us as the *"one called alongside to help,"* he evaluates our true spirit: do we *grieve* him by asking Christ for his power for selfish reasons? How will he react? He will sadly refuse to serve us as the intercessor. He will not make *"groans that words cannot express"*[2] because our desires do not merit his presenting them to Christ. The body also suffers from our selfishness in seeking Christ's power for our own uses.

Again, a body member who should have access with the Holy Spirit's assistance to Christ's inner presence is filled with unrepentance. *Resisting* the Spirit isolates the believer from Christ and also has grave results in responding to the other members of the body. In this case, the Spirit may have to participate in discipline of the rebelling spirit.

To receive the *filling* of the Spirit is an awesome experience, for not only is he present as the agent who does the filling, but the "living water" that floods us is Christ himself! The woman at the well was told he is the living water, and the Holy Spirit is the baptizer.

We rejoice in the many activities of the Holy Spirit:

+ He is in the world, convicting unbelievers and calling them to Christ (John 16:8).
+ He seals the believer at salvation's portal by entering that life along with Christ (Ephesians 4:30).
+ He is our teacher, sharing all Christ has commanded (Luke 12:12).
+ He is our intercessor, the examiner of our thoughts and motives . . . and so much more!

Thus, please be assured that when we replace Christ to his rightful place as the King of Kings and exalt him as the source of all spiritual gifts, it in no way denigrates the Holy Spirit. But when we exalt the Holy Spirit to diminish the role of Christ, the Holy Spirit is the very first one to be grieved.

CHRIST IS THE SOURCE. THE SPIRIT IS THE "MANIFESTER"

A special word is used for the spiritual gifting provided by Christ: *charisma*. Thayer defines the term as "a gift of grace; a favor which one receives without any merit of his own."[3] I would like to propose we adopt this further definition of the term:

Charismata: spiritual gifts manifested as an activity of a believer, directed to perform a supernatural ministry in which Christ releases his power through the activity of the Holy Spirit.

The "energizings" of Christ's gifts are clearly to be performed by every single believer, not just those designated as elders or pastors. This is made clear through scripture:

We have different gifts, according to the grace given us. If a man's gift is prophesying, let him use it in proportion to his faith. If it is serving, let him serve; if it is teaching, let him teach; if it is encouraging, let him encourage; if it is contributing to the needs of others, let him give generously; if it is leadership, let him govern diligently; if it is showing mercy, let him do it cheerfully (Romans 12:6-8).

In 1 Corinthians 12:7, the Spirit *manifests* the gifts. The Greek for this word is *phanerosis*, which describes something "being bestowed,"[4] or "to put something somewhere."[5] Scriptures related to the gifts being *bestowed* all credit the Holy Spirit with the action. But nowhere does Scripture indicate that the *transmitter* is also the *source* of the spiritual gifts:

1 Corinthians 12:7-11: *Now to each one the* manifestation *of the Spirit is given for the common good. To one there is given* through the Spirit *the message of wisdom, to another the message of knowledge* by means of the same Spirit, *to another faith* by the same Spirit, *to another gifts of healing* by that one Spirit, *to another miraculous powers, to another prophecy, to another distinguishing between spirits, to another speaking in different kinds of tongues, and to still another the interpretation of tongues. All these are the work of one and the same Spirit, and he gives them to each one, just as he determines* (my emphasis).

1 Corinthians 12:27-31: *Now you are the body of Christ, and each one of you is a part of it. And in the church God has appointed first of all apostles, second prophets, third teachers, then workers of miracles, also those having gifts of healing, those able to help others, those with gifts of administration, and those speaking in different kinds of tongues. Are all apostles? Are all prophets? Are all teachers? Do all work miracles? Do all have gifts of healing? Do all speak in tongues? Do all interpret? But eagerly desire the greater gifts.*

Schlatter wrote,

It is the Christ's calling to render forgiveness effective by baptizing with the Spirit. *Spirit!* This is another of Jesus' great words that proclaim his majesty and provides his message with profundity. Through the Spirit he cleanses us internally; through the Spirit he teaches us to know God's will, and through the Spirit he produces the desire to do God's will. . . .

He who baptizes with the Spirit acts upon us in the service of divine grace, which has access to our innermost being, and with the royal authority that reigns over a person's life. Therefore he has authority to baptize with the Spirit as well as with fire. Effective, definitive forgiveness cannot be separated from effective, definitive judgment; they are entrusted to the same hand. Because the Christ administers them both, he produces the pure humanity that is united in God.[6]

When one begins to meditate on this relationship between Christ and his present body—carrying it into the individual Christian's fellowship with him—a new paradigm is realized. But first, the filters in place for a century must be removed. This may be a case where we may properly describe Christians as having spiritual cataracts in their eyes!

Keeping the main thing the main thing

For me, this chapter has touched upon the single most important truth for the establishing of authentic Christ's Basic Bodies: until he is crowned Lord, Master, King, Source, Supplier of all, he is not yet Lord of all. He reigns supreme because the Father assigned him to do so!

Let's review these thoughts, one by one:

+ The present body of Christ is formed from the "called-out ones." They are indwelled by Christ, operating under his guidance to do his work redeeming all men everywhere, in every generation, in every culture.

+ Jesus clearly stated, "*All authority in heaven and on earth has been given to me*"[7] He is the source of their life and their power.
+ Ephesians 4:7, 8 expressly teaches that Christ is the source of the supernatural gifts: *He* (Christ) "*gave gifts to men.*"
+ The place of the Holy Spirit is to bring to us all Christ has commanded.[8]
+ Jesus said in John 14:26, "*But the Counselor, the Holy Spirit, whom the Father will send in my name, will teach you all things and will remind you of everything I have said to you.*"

Thus, we must see Christ as the *source* of the gifts and the Holy Spirit as the *transmitter* of them to all the body members who become the *agents* of Christ's activity within his body and their supernatural activities. Newbigen writes:

> We have here the outline of the way in which we are to understand the witness of the church in relation to all the gifts that God has bestowed upon humankind. . . . This passage [John 16:12-15] suggests a Trinitarian model that will guide our thinking as we proceed. The Father is the giver of all things. They all belong rightly to the Son. It will be the work of the Holy Spirit to guide the church through the course of history into the truth as a whole by taking all God's manifold gifts given to all humankind and declaring their true meaning to the church as that which belongs to the Son. The end to which it all looks is "*a plan for the fullness of time, to unite all things to him, things in heaven and things on earth*" (Eph. 1:10).[9]

WHAT DIFFERENCE DOES IT MAKE?

To the reader who says, "Why not go on believing that the Holy Spirit is the source and also the supplier?" the answer is very pointed: we must understand the true nature of the body of Christ. To do that, we must abandon a wrong theology defining the *ekklesia*.

The true *ekklesia* is Christ's new body. He does not just empower the people who compose the members of his new community, he is embodied within it! He is the presence manifested as the Holy Spirit distributes spiritual gifts. Consider these two passages:

> Acts 3:6: *Then Peter said, 'Silver or gold I do not have, but what I have I give you. In the name of Jesus Christ of Nazareth, walk.'*

> Acts 16:18: *Paul became so troubled that he turned around and said to the spirit, 'In the name of Jesus Christ I command you to come out of her!'*

In both instances, as Peter and Paul manifested the gifts of healing and expulsion of demons, it was done *"in the name of Jesus Christ."* The source is clearly Christ, not the Holy Spirit. Yet it is obvious that the Holy Spirit was the agent who caused the power of Christ to flow.

The community is in Christ . . . and Christ is in the community!

The *Gospel* we must declare is that the Spirit of Christ *literally inhabits* the spirit of every believer. Christ is the one who has all power in heaven and on earth. He is the revealer of the Godhead. He brings with him the fullness of the Godhead to indwell every Christian. He is the Resurrected One who has led captivity captive. He is the one who is seated in the heavenly places. Paul said it so clearly in Colossians 3:11: *"Christ is all, and is in all."*

The spiritual residence of God on the earth today is Christ himself—not Christ alone, but Christ in his new body, the *ekklesia*, Christ's Basic Bodies. The community exists first of all as the basic body. It then relates to all the rest of the indwelled bodies to become the complete witness of Christ all over the earth. We need to expel from our paradigms every other concept of what the Christ-indwelled community is all about. It is not Christ divided into a hundred thousand fragments: there is only one Christ. It is one Christ in all the Christ's Baisc Bodies that together compose the total body of Christ on the earth today.

The corruption of the historical church

Breaking with the past is the only way to leave behind the corruption that has been created by the historical church, rightly observed with cynicism by the general public. Seen as a subculture, the witness of traditional Christianity before the watching world is mediocre. Cynical unbelievers ask, "Where is the Lord God of miracles?" The splintered church life, the competition, the lack of true unity, the loss of his power in their activities, is obvious to all who observe from the outside. When will we admit the reality?

The true work of the Holy Spirit in our generation—his activity in choosing and baptizing believers into the body of Christ so they will reveal God at work in true community—is not properly honored. The true community is yeast within the bread of society, exposing the supernatural presence and power of the eternal Christ.

There are so many riches contained in our Lord! Christ is much greater than what we have experienced. There is no theme that occurs with greater frequency in the New Testament than the phrase "in Christ," used 87 times. The reference to "Lord" appears 680 times.

We must fully grasp what it means to be dwelling in Christ and for him to be dwelling in us. He must become our atmosphere. Milt Rodriguez writes:

> I know it may sound silly, but could you think of yourself as living in a bubble? Have you heard of someone who must live inside of a plastic bubble because he is too prone to disease due to a weak immune system? He has his own private environment that protects him from the dangers in the world. The private

"bubble" contains everything that he needs to live in this world without becoming contaminated by it. His air, food, water, etc., are all contained within the plastic bubble and he only relates to the world through the plastic container. This is a poor example of what it is like to be in Christ. Everything you need is inside of Him. Indeed, all the riches of God are inside of Him. Because we are in Him, we also have access to all those things that are in Him. Isn't that amazing?[10]

FELLOWSHIP WITH THE INDWELLING CHRIST

It is only a beginning when we focus our whole thought life on what Christ thinks, to let our eyes see what he sees, to feel the emotions he feels as he observes others around us.

Daily devotional times cause us to approach the "God Most High" for only a small fraction of our day. However, communion with the indwelling Christ is Paul's passion: *"Pray continually; give thanks in all circumstances, for this is God's will for you in Christ Jesus."*[11] Constant fellowship with the indwelling Christ guarantees that we "walk worthy of the Lord, fully pleasing Him, being fruitful in every good work and increasing in the knowledge of God."[12]

We have much to learn! What happens to a person when life in the "bubble" becomes a reality? What happens to Christ's Basic Bodies when body members step over the line from being a man-organized group to a Christ-empowered group? How do we begin such a journey? Where are the examples of this taking place?

Communing with Christ

The answer is obvious. We must learn to commune with Christ. We must be sensitive to the way he speaks, to how our ears listen. To be sure, we will experience the full impact of the Spirit interceding with groans that words cannot express.

I have experienced two profound experiences of being with persons I sensed lived in the presence of Christ. Perhaps sharing these examples will help you begin your journey:

The first experience was my visit with Corrie Ten Boom, author of *The Hiding Place*.[13] We were seated backstage in a South Carolina auditorium, waiting for the start of an evening service where we both were to speak. As I asked about her history, her lips were continually moving. At first I thought this elderly Dutch-speaking woman was repeating my English words. I finally realized that was not the case. I said, "Miss Corrie, what were you whispering to yourself?" She waved her hand and said, "Ach, my son, you must not be concerned about an old woman. I was just talking to Jesus about our visit with you."

The second experience took place in Hong Kong. I was introduced to a woman who had spent many years alone and tortured in a China prison. She had recently been released and was adjusting to her new environment. She was hesitant to answer my interview questions about her incarceration, answering with brief comments. I felt I should not probe. I finally said, "My sister in Christ, will you pray a blessing over me?" As she began to pray in Chinese, I was aware that Christ was powerfully present with us. She had such a close tie to him! He had been her only companion for years and her intimacy with him was obvious as she prayed.

Our communion with the indwelling Christ must become our pathway into the next mighty move of God on this planet. It will take time to develop this intimacy with Christ. We must always remember that "where two or three are gathered," he is in the midst.

When Christ's Basic Bodies experience the true activity of Christ manifested in their midst, it is an awesome experience. Several years ago I was ministering in Almaty, Kazakhestan. Seated on a sheepskin, I addressed a circle of women who had come from a small village to hear me speak. In talking about strongholds, I was prompted to speak of daughters who had been molested by their own fathers as an example.

One precious young mother spoke privately to me afterwards. She said, "I was constantly raped by my father as a child, beginning at age seven. My mother told me she would beat me if I told anyone, and she did nothing to stop it. I have hated and despised my father for many years. This has ruined my ability to be close to my husband. Since becoming a Christian I know I must forgive him, but I cannot! What must I do?"

I replied, "You are a member of Christ's body. The Scripture says we are to confess such things one to another so that the entire body can minister until he brings healing. Would you be willing to share this with the sisters in your group?"

I sat outside the circle as she began to share for the first time all the details of her hurt and her inability to forgive. The women all wept as the terrible story unfolded.

I spoke through my interpreter: "My sisters, now begin to pray that Christ will rise up within you. You are the body of Christ. The one who prayed on the cross, 'Father, forgive them,' dwells in you. What we are unable to forgive in our own strength can be replaced by his power to forgive. Pray with your sister that his forgiveness will rise up within her." As they simultaneously prayed aloud, this precious woman gave a loud cry and collapsed. The women sat surrounding her, praying softly. For more than twenty minutes she remained quiet as the Lord ministered to her. When her eyes opened, the joy of heaven was on her face! She said, "It's gone! The hate is gone!"

As Christ's Basic Bodies learn through such events, gradually their focus on Christ becomes more intense. So does the manifestation of Christ's power. Frank Laubach wrote,

One question now to be put to the test is this: Can we have the contact with God all the time? All the time awake, fall asleep in His arms, and awaken in His presence? Can we attain that? Can we do His will all the time? Can we think His thoughts all the time?[14]

Charles Carrin has said:

It's time for a move to the next level. We must pray every day
that God will increase our anointing and make better use of us.
Our prime of church life is not in where we have been. It is the
point where the power of the Holy Spirit will become the
strongest. Unless we will press into God, we will never reach
that final destination. The moment we think we have "arrived,"
we will miss the "more."[15]

A final question

How are your filters working? I recently sat by a man on a flight to
Houston who explained he travels the world helping oil companies
produce more oil out of their wells. He explained his job was to change
the paradigms of the men who serviced the wells. Instead of just taking
down the information from the gauges, he inspires creativity so they
will begin to tweak the system of pipes to produce more pressure,
drawing more oil from the ground. He explained that even a seven
percent increase can generate millions of dollars of profit.

This man is paid a huge salary just to help the employees "see" what
they do not see, even when it is right before their eyes. In fact, he has
created a T-shirt that he gives to those who "catch on" as he tutors them.
It says, "Brother, can you spare a paradigm?"

Make yourself such a T-shirt! If you don't want to wear it in public,
sleep in it. Maybe it will help you dream of a church that is to come, a
church that will be so Christ-empowered it will overwhelm the
kingdoms of this world with his kingdom. After all, it *does* dwell in his
Basic Body!

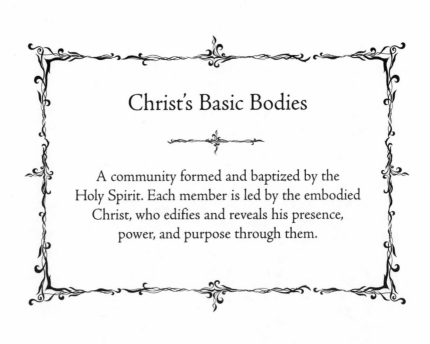

Christ's Basic Bodies

A community formed and baptized by the
Holy Spirit. Each member is led by the embodied
Christ, who edifies and reveals his presence,
power, and purpose through them.

There's More, So Much More!

And let us consider one another in order to stir up love and good works, not forsaking the assembling of ourselves together, as is the manner of some, but exhorting one another, and so much the more as you see the Day approaching.　　　　　　　　　　　　　(Hebrews 10:24, 25, NKJV)

Therefore strengthen the hands which hang down, and the feeble knees, and make straight paths for your feet, so that what is lame may not be dislocated, but rather be healed.　　　　　　　　　　(Hebrews 12:12, 13, NKJV)

Dr. Penrose St. Amant spoke in our seminary class about the way it takes just three generations for a vision to turn to ice. He remarked that Luther was the "man on fire" who had such passion for what God had shown him that he threw an ink well at the devil. But, as my friend Bill Beckham often comments, "Movements are messy." I waded through the literature penned by Luther's disciple, Melanchthon, and found he proceeded to systematize Luther's fire into an intellectual ice cube. Then came the third generation . . . all they had to copy was Melanchthon, and dry rot sat in that could never be used for tinder. The fire had completely burned out.

By the time Hebrews was written about 65 A.D., the third generation of believers had appeared and dry rot had set into community life. The verses above refer to Christ's Basic Bodies where body members no longer looked to the interest of others.[1] It didn't take long for the plan of God to be negated by the independent, self-serving spirits of men who did not understand the importance of community life in the kingdom of God.

The deterioration of community as a lifestyle came even earlier to the Galatian church, where the "leaven of the Pharisees" gained control over them. The Corinthian church was also filled with carnality (*sarkikos*), and lost its way. They were warned that "not discerning the body" was a step toward death. In Revelation 1-3, we see the communities at the end of the first century at the final levels of deterioration.

By the end of the first century, John looked with sadness at the state of the seven churches in Asia, and Christ stood in the midst of them with warnings of what would happen if they did not repent. William Shakespeare caught the drift of all this: "To-morrow, and to-morrow, and to-morrow, creeps in this petty pace from day to day, to the last syllable of recorded time."[2]

IS THERE ANY HOPE FOR THIS GENERATION?

After centuries, we are still man-centered in our view of how the Christian life should be lived. We seek spiritual power as a personal asset, rather than seeking the source of that power and submitting ourselves to be channels of Christ's life and grace gifts.

There's more: Acts 3:1-10

The third chapter of Acts begins abruptly without providing any idea of the amount of time intervening between the incident on the day of Pentecost and the subsequent events.

Luke brings an account of Peter and John going to the temple at the hour of prayer. We have no complete record of all the wonders and signs that were done through the apostles in the opening period of the new community. However, we do have a report of the lame man who was at the Beautiful Gate of the temple.

Evidently, Luke selected this particular miracle to teach us something very significant. This was more than a miracle; it was a sign

(4:22) in which a picture was given in the physical of what could be done in the spiritual. Just as a man was made whole physically (4:9-12), so in Christ one could also be made whole spiritually.

Peter and John went to the temple at three o'clock in the afternoon, the usual time of prayer for the Jews. (Perhaps these apostles remembered that Christ died on the cross at three o'clock in the afternoon.) Along their journey they came upon a forty year old man who was lame from birth.

The verbs in the Greek indicate that the man asked Peter and John for money while he was still being carried by friends or family. The first words of Peter must been disappointing to him: *"Silver or gold I do not have."*

Why did they think he was coming to the temple day after day if it was not to receive silver or gold? What else could he use to buy bread? Fine speeches could not satisfy a gnawing hunger or clothe a man against the evening chill. And what could these men give that would be better than silver or gold?

But Simon Peter said, "Look at us!" This indicated the man's eyes were wandering and his words were mechanically addressed to them. Peter's command surely aroused a sense of expectation from this lame man. This man expected to receive something, in all probability, money.

When Peter had the lame man's attention, he did two things: first, he admitted he was financially bankrupt: *"Silver or gold I do not have."* Then, Peter demonstrated an amazing wealth in the spiritual realm: *"In the name of Jesus Christ of Nazareth, walk."*

Walk? This man never walked! He had been lame from birth. When you tell a lame man over forty who had never placed his foot on the ground to walk, you might as well tell a worm to fly!

The name of Jesus as used here was not a magic formula used to produce a miracle. Rather, Peter was saying, "Christ is the power I possess. I'm not depending on silver and gold. In fact, money is not your greatest need. I have said, 'In the name of Jesus,' so when you walk, you will know who healed you. It is to him you owe your gratitude."

Undoubtedly, this beggar didn't feel he had a physical need that could be changed. His condition was, in his mind, permanent. His objective was to beg for money, food, and clothing. But that is not what Peter offered him. Instead, he offered him the power and physical healing of Jesus.

When Simon Peter said, *"In the name of Jesus Christ of Nazareth, walk"* he took the beggar by his hand and pulled him to his feet. Scripture reports, "and instantly the man's feet and ankles became strong." In that very moment, this man who had never been able to stand or walk felt a strange strength in his legs and feet; they actually supported him instead of collapsing beneath him.

There is no "if" or "maybe"; there is no slow recovery. We all know that even when legs are sound a human being cannot suddenly walk, leap, or jump. Walking is an acquired skill. But this lame man didn't need to learn. He walked perfectly from the first moment. Strength came into his feet and ankle bones. He leaped up, then stood, then walked, then entered the temple. The man's body bounded with newfound energy; his soul was flooded with divine joy and praise. His limbs were agile and active. He was expressing his indescribable emotions. Who can even imagine this man's feelings?

Remember, it was money the man was seeking, but it was a miracle of healing he received. He was only asking for some money to get through the day, but he received his legs for life.

Note the amazing effect the lame man's healing had upon the people: *"When all the people saw him walking and praising God, they recognized him as the same man who used to sit begging at the temple gate called Beautiful, and they were filled with wonder and amazement at what had happened to him"* (Acts 3:9, 10). The people were immediately convinced beyond the shadow of doubt that God was at work.

There is a lame, crippled, sick society lying at our door, unable to be the kind of men and women and young people that God wants them to be. And as the healing hand of Jesus Christ is laid again and again in our hearts and our lives, we are being made whole, as God intended us to be. This is the great message we need to declare today: "In the name of Jesus Christ of Nazareth, rise up and walk, and be what God wants you to be." In his name and by his power, the lame are still made to walk, the blind still receive their sight, and the selfish turn their wealth to world need. The immoral find purity, and the lost are saved![3]

THE "MORE" WE MUST HAVE

"What I have I give you." (Acts 3:6)

The lame, crippled, sick, and lost of our world must see God at work in us. Weak and helpless and hopeless mankind is in need of the transforming, healing, life-changing power, which comes to those who place their trust in Christ. And, we as a community must stretch out our hand in loving ministry, to offer relief and to express our love and concern, but we must do so "in the name of Jesus Christ." We must inspire faith in him alone who can heal and save.

The prophet Joel's promise was partially fulfilled at Pentecost.[4] The community of the "last days" is still to come. It will be a time when the total community will be empowered by Christ to *prophesy*.[5] Note those in the community to be empowered: "all people" . . . "sons and daughters" . . . "old men" . . . "young men" . . . "servants, both men and women." This is an awesome description of what the "more" will be like. The totality of the body of Christ will be energized to reveal his inner life.

To effect this, Paul described the equippers who must be in place: apostles, prophets, evangelists, pastors, teachers.[6] It seems to be seldom emphasized that the one who appoints these is not the Holy Spirit, but Christ! How much plainer could Paul make this truth?

There is one body and one Spirit, just as you were called in one hope of your calling; one Lord, one faith, one baptism: one God and Father of all, who is above all, and through all, and in you all. But to each one of us grace was given according to the measure of Christ's gift. Therefore He says: "When He ascended on high, He led captivity captive, And gave gifts to men." (Now this, "He ascended"—what does it mean but that He also first descended into the lower parts of the earth? He who descended is also the One who ascended far above all the heavens, that He might fill all things.) And He Himself gave some to be apostles, some prophets, some evangelists, and some pastors and teachers, for the equipping of the saints for the work of ministry, for the edifying of the body of Christ, till we all come to the unity of the faith and of the knowledge of the Son of God, to a perfect man, to the measure of the stature of the fullness of Christ; that we should no longer be children, tossed to and fro and carried about with every wind of doctrine, by the trickery of men, in the cunning craftiness of deceitful plotting, but, speaking the truth in love, may grow up in all things into Him who is the head—Christ—from whom the whole body, joined and knit together by what every joint supplies, according to the effective working by which every part does its share, causes growth of the body for the edifying of itself in love.[7]

The formation of authentic Christ's Basic Bodies must begin with the functioning of this fivefold body of equippers properly positioned to equip all believers. This creates a serious problem for the traditional church. That problem is the role of the senior pastor:

There's no room at the top!

We have casually ignored the New Testament structures for life in community. Church planting apostles and elders fulfilled the roles of equipping the body for ministry. The elders were those selected as the fivefold servants within each body. There were no senior pastors!

Let me be clear: I am defining the role (not merely the title) of a senior pastor (as opposed to a lead pastor, defined below) as a credentialed professional clergyman who is given full control of a congregation. He is given absolute power to direct all details, to preach all sermons, and to

preside over all events with little or no accountability to others for his decisions. He is in all
respects "king of the castle." Other staff
members are given limited authority as they
serve under his rule. The congregation, in
turn, expects him to grow the structure
successfully. And then, when he's proved himself
in his current congregation as a professional, he
moves on to become the senior pastor of a larger, more
prestigious congregation (enjoying all the perks that come with it).

There is no "cow" in organized religion as sacred as the belief that
senior pastors have reached the pinnacle of Christian service. Sadly, this
is a worldwide attitude. It has been embedded in all traditional views of
the church for centuries.

The exalted position of the celebrated "senior pastor" must go to the
cross before the last days community can take shape! Nothing is as
crippling to the body of Christ today than the replacement of the
fivefold ministries with the celebrated senior pastor position. The
tragedy is that for every exalted man behind a pulpit, there are scores of
people sitting in pews, looking past backs of heads toward his
passionate face, listening to endless teaching that fails to provide any
significant equipping for their precious ministries.

The pressures on this man are horrendous. Dropouts from
the positions of senior pastors are at an all-time high. Sunscape
Re-Creation Ministries of Colorado, a ministry serving clergy in crises,
quotes George Barna's report that in all denominations nationwide,
1,600 ministers per month are terminated or forced to resign. Although a
sense of hurt is unavoidable for both pastor and congregation, it is
particularly traumatic for a minister who steps down.[8] *That represents
19,200 clergymen a year!* A conversation with a staff member at
Sunscape reflected the stresses of men who seek to be the entire fivefold
structure by themselves burn out quickly.

Theological seminaries concentrate on preparing pastors and educational directors and worship leaders for predictable tasks. Billions of dollars have been invested in these institutions. They are the tails that wag the dogs, propagating the structures that must be transformed. Would Jesus look at seminaries and say, "Beware of the leaven of the Pharisees"?

The power of the senior pastor has frequently been exposed in scores of seminars I have held through the years. Hundreds of staff pastors have told me they were sent by the senior pastor to attend the conference, but he himself was not interested in participating in cell group life. They asked, "How will this concept function if the senior pastor does not participate?" I had no choice but to tell them I cannot find one example of a church transitioning from programs to cell life successfully when the senior pastor did not participate! Numerous examples come to my mind of staff pastors who have been "brought on board" to develop a small group structure while the senior pastor watched from afar. Over and over, these men failed to see transformational change.

THE CRUCIAL IMPORTANCE OF THE "LEAD PASTOR"

Am I suggesting there should be a structure where there is no key pastor to lead a congregation of Christ's Basic Bodies? Not at all! The notion that there can be plural leadership of a congregation by elders without a lead pastor is not possible.

I personally know of five churches in Houston who attempted rule by a multiple eldership in which all had equal votes in decisionmaking. Every one of these churches dissolved. The problem in each case was that one foot-dragging elder could stall decisions not to his liking, usually by piously commenting, "We haven't prayed enough about this! We cannot do this." Thus, the laggard rules the majority by his one negative vote.

The term "lead pastor" does not define the traditional role of a "senior pastor" described above. The contrasts may not be readily grasped, but it is crucial to understand the differences.

Every effective body of Christ *must* have an anointed lead pastor whose authority is bestowed by Christ and is so recognized by all. He will delight to see the expansion of the contributions made by the fivefold servants who share in the equipping and preaching.

A senior pastor serves as a CEO with total control over all details of the structure. The pastoral staff are subordinate to him and follow his instructions exactly. There is no room for joint development of the structure, which is controlled by the head man. In contrast, a lead pastor serves as a developer of others, encouraging the gifts and talents of his pastoral team, constantly seeking to release them to grow the single vision of the community.

A lead pastor is a visionary who leads through a unified team of co-workers, always discerning how each person's ministry contributes to the vision. *He personally participates in a Christ's Basic Body.* He is not threatened by the strengths and gifting of those who serve with him to equip believers in Christ's Basic Bodies ... he feels privileged to lead them and is accountable for his own life to them.

Further, a lead pastor sees no divisions between "clergy" and "laity." Instead of a formal church staff and supporting church members, he sees every believer as a minister to be developed to the fullest level of servanthood. Those entering the community are given a "boot camp" experience to prepare them for service. The traditional limitations of church life that restrict the creative expression of artists, writers, musicians, and others are removed. All of life is opened to become a place of exalting the person of Christ through talents and skills.

For example

I know of many examples of the teamwork developed by communities who have a lead pastor. One outstanding example is the Mosaic ministry in Los Angeles, California, guided by Erwin McManus. He proposes a theology that believes the message does not change but our methods should change.

Most significant is the formation of Mosaic's internal "seminary" in conjunction with Golden Gate Baptist Theological Seminary. Hand-picked students blend traditional cognitive courses taught by the seminary professors with practical assignments within the life of Mosaic. Thus, Mosaic is equipping a future generation of lead pastors. The environment these students experience as they take their formal training guarantees they will propagate a new pattern of ecclesiology into the next generation.

While he is a brilliant communicator, McManus shares the platforms of his many celebration services with other preaching pastors. He himself lives in a limelight as an author and speaker, but he is always involving the community he leads. When speaking in other places, he takes both fellow pastors and seminary students with him. He personifies life lived in Christ's body.

As a lead pastor, McManus now mentors many other communities around the world. The development of groups as the heart of the ministry and the formation of team leadership has marked this Los Angeles congregation as a model for those on other continents.

The future of the body of Christ must begin to replace the oligarchy of a senior pastor with the servant ministry of the lead pastor. How long will this transition take? Let us pray that the acceleration of this trend will be faster and faster! Little future exists for the senior pastor model.

HOW THE FIVEFOLD DEVELOPS

In the New Testament, each community formed by the apostles was allowed to mature for a period of about two years. Often the founders moved away to plant in another city. Gradually the unmonitored group saw spiritual maturity in those who manifested the spiritual strengths of the fivefold ministries. These were then observed by the visiting apostles and appointed as elders. These became the fivefold equippers. They rose like cream in milk to the top, but always served from the bottom to build up the body.

Paul observed those in the communities who had the calling of the apostle, and mentored them by taking them with him in his travels: *"He was accompanied by Sopater son of Pyrrhus from Berea, Aristarchus and Secundus from Thessalonica, Gaius from Derbe, Timothy also, and Tychicus and Trophimus from the province of Asia"* (Acts 20:4).

Those who were prophets seemed to reside within local communities and possibly were itinerant as well: Agabus was from Judea but met Paul in Caesarea (Acts 21:10). The so-called fivefold servants are all given to prepare body members for active ministry.[9]

Sarah was a young businesswoman with a Catholic background and a former church dropout. She attended a cell group for singles I led. She was a quiet lady, listening deeply and speaking little. After five weeks with us, I asked her to share her spiritual journey with the group. She replied, "Last week at the close of the meeting, I surrendered my life to Christ. I wanted to see if my commitment would make a difference and be visible to others, so I did not say anything. I have had a week to experience Christ's life in me, and it is real. I am truly his child."

Sarah was a magnet, drawing friend after friend to the single's group, helping them surrender to Christ. In fact, she single-handedly caused the group to grow so large it multiplied into two groups. I kept her with me when the multiplication took place, and within four more months she had filled up a second group with new believing friends.

I thought to myself, "This lady is solidly surrendered to the Lord. I will invite her to become a cell group leader." When I approached her, she responded with a frown: "Ralph, let me pray about that."

A few days later she contacted me and commented, "Thank you for the encouragement to lead a group, but I sense the Lord wants me to decline. I do not have the same gifting you and the other facilitators possess. He has called me to bring people to follow him. I guess I am like Andrew, who told others he had found Jesus."

At that time in my own understanding of how Christ's Basic Body functioned, I had made two errors. The first one was not to discern that within the fivefold ministries, the gift of evangelism is as crucial as the gift of the apostle, prophet, pastor, or teacher. It was my thinking back then that the greatest calling would be to lead a group. I was wrong!

My second error was in assuming that my role as a leader gave me the privilege of recommending what others should do to serve Christ. He had his own plan for Sarah and she listened to his voice instead of mine!

THE FIVEFOLD MINISTERS DEVELOP IN CHRIST'S BODIES NATURALLY

Months ago, a team serving in my local body realized the biblical basis for multiple leadership. As the planting apostle, I knew too much focus was placed on my role. I immediately began to restructure key areas that would play down the concept the congregation had that I was, if not the senior pastor, at least the lead pastor. I did this by sharing the pulpit with members of the congregation who were maturing in their journey.

We also shared with the body all we had learned about the place of the fivefold ministries. It was obvious that in the early church these people floated to the top of body life, as cream does in milk. That is why Paul told Titus and others to return to churches planted two or more years earlier to appoint elders.[10] By then, those who would fill the fivefold ministry positions would be obvious. Without the smothering effect of the apostles dominating those communities, Christ raised up those whose capacities suited them for the equipping of the believers. We really can trust Christ to empower his body!

What, then, does the role of the Christian leader involve? To operate like Jesus did with his disciples. He provided them with teaching, to be sure—but far beyond the words he gave them were the *experiences* he provided for them. This is our task: to provide *active involvement over time* that will reshape old values and install new ones. He walked on water and drew Peter to try it out. He called Lazarus from the tomb and sent them to raise the dead. He prayed all night and had them experience this with him.

Traditionally, a good Christian leader prepares sermons or instructive messages as his primary role for the congregation. Yet if we read aloud all the words of Jesus—using a harmony of the Gospels so we do not duplicate them—it can be done in less than ninety-five minutes (try it!).

The balance of the four gospels report the *experiences* Jesus provided to his disciples. He lived with them and established by his own life the values they needed to absorb. This is the major missing ingredient in church life today. The curse of the platform elevating the hired holy man above the masses has destroyed kingdom life.

The fivefold ministry focuses on *values and tasks.* Like flight instructors, they will be at the side of potential apostle, prophet, evangelist, pastor, and teacher. They will say, "Watch what I do and the way I do it." "Now, you try it while I watch." "Now, let me send you out without me to do it and report back." "Now, I send you as the Father sent me."

FIVEFOLD MINISTERS ARE FACILITATORS, NOT LECTURERS

Christian schools (particularly seminaries) fail to focus those being prepared for "full-time ministry" to be facilitators. Instead, the institutions concentrate heavily on the cognitive domain of learning. This has made it nearly impossible to plant core values and develop spiritual skills in others. This must change!

I seek to teach others these basic truths about facilitating:
+ Provide an experience.
+ Secure feedback.
+ "Feed back" the feedback.
+ Probe for the principle established.
+ Provide another experience, and so forth.

It takes six experiences to install a value that will remain in those equipped. *It takes six to stick!* But it takes more than the experiences, it takes an equipper with the passion of Jesus to patiently live with and further develop those who have not yet grasped truth.

The journey to wholeness will take the length of our lives. At the close of this life, we will have completed all the "boot camp" training. We will be evaluated by God's "personnel committee" at the Bema judgment for assignment in his coming kingdom. Those who were faithful over much will be recognized and given responsible tasks to perform.

Yes, *there's more!* Will you become a part of the search for it?

Where to begin

One of the first steps to take is to gather a group together who are visionaries and begin to discuss the issues in the chapters of this book. Together, you can form a Christ's Basic Body. Invest much of your time learning how to commune with him as a body. Learn about each other by bearing one another's burdens and seeking the Spirit's presence as a carrier of your groaning to his throne. Then, return with the King's empowerment to fulfill his mission on the earth.

All this theory must be fleshed out. When it becomes flesh and blood, he will exalt himself through you. Remember, before the foundations of the earth you were chosen to be in him and he in you. Before your mother gave birth to you, the Holy Spirit was preparing to summon you to enter the kingdom. Your flesh and blood are not your own. It belongs first to Christ and then to those to whom the Spirit will join you through a supernatural baptism. As you are submerged into his authentic body, expect to experience the supernatural events that churchianity either fakes or rejects. For every counterfeit there is an original.

Doesn't your very being cry out for this experience? It is costly. It will cost you your life. You will understand Paul's heart when he wrote in Acts 20:23, 24,

I only know that in every city the Holy Spirit warns me that prison and hardships are facing me. However, I consider my life worth nothing to me, if only I may finish the race and complete the task the Lord Jesus has given me—the task of testifying to the gospel of God's grace.

Life had only begun when I gave Him my heart,
'Twas the dawn of the day, it was only the start,
God's law was satisfied by His Son crucified,
I was saved, was reborn in my heart.
But there's more, so much more than that first sweet day,
More, so much more ev'ry passing day.
For the life I now live God is living through me
In each word, in each deed, each day.
—*Robert Oldenburg*

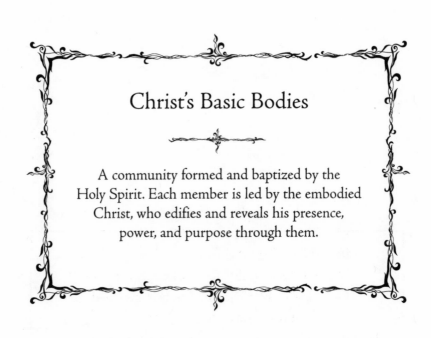

Christ's Basic Bodies

A community formed and baptized by the
Holy Spirit. Each member is led by the embodied
Christ, who edifies and reveals his presence,
power, and purpose through them.

chapter fifteen

Here's the Baton
Will You Run With It?

Do you not know that in a race all the runners run, but only one gets the prize? Run in such a way as to get the prize. Everyone who competes in the games goes into strict training. They do it to get a crown that will not last; but we do it to get a crown that will last forever. Therefore I do not run like a man running aimlessly; I do not fight like a man beating the air. No, I beat my body and make it my slave so that after I have preached to others, I myself will not be disqualified for the prize. (1 Corinthians 9:24-27)

Therefore, since we are surrounded by such a great cloud of witnesses, let us throw off everything that hinders and the sin that so easily entangles, and let us run with perseverance the race marked out for us. (Hebrews 12:1)

I just learned that my Wheaton roommate from 1948 has gone to be with the King. I shall never forget when Jim Rust ran the mile relay race with coach Gil Dodds, world-champion miler, shouting on the edge of the track. At the top of his lungs, Dodds clamored, "Jim, pull the chain! Flush it! Flush it!" And flush it he did. He left the competition in the dust nearly every time. It seemed that his sinewy frame knew no exhaustion.

Back in our room in Culp Hall, I would admire the growing collection of gold and silver medals he placed on the top of his dresser. One day as we were praying together, Jim said, "Ralph, you know the race I *really* want to win?" "What is it, Jim?" I replied.

Opening his well-used Bible, he turned to these words in 2 Timothy 4:7, 8:

I have fought the good fight, I have finished the race, I have kept the faith. Now there is in store for me the crown of righteousness, which the Lord, the righteous Judge, will award to me on that day—and not only to me, but also to all who have longed for his appearing.

Pointing to the top of the dresser, he said, "They are just baubles. I'm going for the *real* gold."

Dear Jim! You have gone to the winner's stand. The *Shekinah* fire burned up all the baubles as your life was examined. But the gold, silver, and precious stones you received were earned as you put up with this freshman who shared your room and your heart. You never left an imprint on anyone more deeply than me!

Although Ruth, my wife, encourages me to "never say never," at my late age (born on April Fools' Day in 1929) I feel this will be my "last hurrah" as a writer of books. I am passionate about all that has been written on these pages. I would rejoice if that passion has rubbed off on you! It is my earnest prayer that this book will make an imprint on you.

ABOUT YOUR FILTERS

How have you accommodated your filters? How far did you get before they began to limit what you were able to see?

+ **Awareness?** Give this book away to someone who might read it.
+ **Willing to Receive?** Get curious and ask around. You may find others like yourself.
+ **Controlled Attention?** Don't attend another of those seminars your expense account allows you to attend! They are all trying to patch old wineskins.
+ **Commitment?** Wow! Sure hope you have a vision that can pay the price of rejection. It goes with the territory, but it's worth it, I assure you.
+ **Characterization?** Go for it! You'll be controlled by an inner passion

that will wake you up with a determination to find the way to the pure body of Christ. Your best friends will be Christ and the Holy Spirit. And the Father will whisper, "Beloved adopted son, I am JHWH — I will always be for you what I have always been!"

Like flakes of skin after you have been sunburned, you will find your filters peel off gradually, not all at once. You can expect that, depending on what filter you are now dealing with, God will continue to speak to you about the passion of his heart: the body he desires for his Son to embody.

You will begin to see new *interpretations of Scripture* you have read through filters for many years. These are truly Aha! moments. I have received them for years. The plural use of "you" in the Greek is one example, as I realized how much Paul wrote to the community rather than to the individual. Or, the understanding that the "salvation" mentioned in Philippians 2:12 is to be experienced in body life, where God is working corporately in the members.

UPSTAIRS—DOWNSTAIRS

Not long ago, I suddenly saw something new in the John 3 passage about how Jesus was speaking "upstairs"—from the supernatural environment of the kingdom of God—and playing a mind game with Nicodemus. His thought processes were totally limited to the "downstairs" world of nature and religion. Jesus spoke of birth, wind, and Moses. He must have been greatly amused by Nicodemus' filters that kept him puzzled over Jesus' comments. Nicodemus' filters had moved from *unawareness* to *awareness* to *willingness to receive*. There we leave him . . . Are you at that level right now?

If so, be alert for what *circumstances* suddenly add to your journey as your filters allow new values to be accepted. Think of Nicodemus. He went away with his experience with Jesus plaguing his every activity as a Pharisee.

We see him again trying to endorse Jesus in John 7:50, 51, suffering rebuke by his peers. Something had leaked through his filters! When the Lord was in danger, he chose to speak up. This reveals his move to some level of *commitment* to Jesus.

Through the circumstances in his life, he moved from *unawareness* to *awareness* to *willingness to receive* to *commitment*. The life-changing events of this man who previously could not "see" the kingdom of God drew him to the dead body of Jesus (John 19:39) with seventy-five pounds of embalming spices as he helped place him in a tomb. Would you say he had reached the level of *characterization*?

"Brother, can you spare a paradigm?"

I complete this book with only a brief glimpse of what the end time *ekklesia* will be like. As Christian religion has done for centuries, Christ's Basic Body will face rejection by those who wish to protect their investments in existing structures. Eric Hoffer mentions in *The True Believer* that those with greatest reserves in the present systems will not be the ones to endorse radical change. If your filters repeatedly warn you that to participate in the church of the future will require you to go back to "zero," you will either discard this vision of tomorrow or stand aside and watch those with less to risk carry it forward.

I end this book with a plea to those who have the power and the reputation within existing church structures: this new form of church life will not happen in a hurry. Chances are you may not live to see it happen (I know I won't). So, even though you will not be one of those I encourage to gather a group and start to experience this new lifestyle, don't grieve the Holy Spirit by fighting what you cannot do yourself.

From time to time I find an older pastor of a fine and polished church with plenty of assets who is a visionary. He will endorse and assist financially a young "turk" on his staff to venture on his own and test a new form of church life. Now, that's real kingdom spirit at work!

I want to leave you with the motto that Ruth and I have lived by for nearly all our years together. It has never failed us, and it will not fail you:

It is the task of a servant to obey his Master.
It is the obligation of that Master to provide the servant's resources.
Therefore, the servant shall never lack what he needs!

— The beginning end.

End Notes

Introduction

[1] Years ago, I found a survey that indicated a large group of Americans would choose a funeral home over a church building for their funeral services. This got me thinking. If a person wouldn't be caught dead in a church building, why would they go to one when they were alive?

[2] Neighbour, Ralph, *The Seven Last Words of the Church* (Grand Rapids: Zondervan Publishing Company, 1973).

[3] *Ekklesia* will be further discussed. It is Greek for "called-out people," the source of the English word *church*.

[4] *Ecclesiology* is a term theologians use to describe views of church life.

Chapter One

[1] Malachi 3:10.

[2] 1 Corinthians 1:12; 1 Corinthians 12:13.

[3] Philippians 2:4.

[4] Milt Rodriguez, *The Corporate God*, *The Rebuilder Gazette*, March 14, 2005, http://admin@therebuilders.org.

[5] John 17:11.

[6] 1 John 5:6-8, *NKJV*.

[7] 1 Corinthians 12.

[8] Matthew 18:20. In the case of "two," Christ is the third.

[9] How can the word "church" as used today ever be used to define this truth?

[10] Philippians 2:4.

[11] 1 Corinthians 12:13 specifically and the entire chapter as well.

[12] Hebrews 13:8.

[13] Manfred Haller, *The Mystery of God, : Christ All In and in All*, (The Rebuilders: http://therebuilders.org, 2004,), Foreword.

[14] Acts 2:17.

[15] Philippians 2:4; I 1 Corinthians 14:24-25.

[16] *Oikos*: "the inmates of a house, all the persons forming one family, a household" (from *Thayer's Greek Lexicon*, Electronic Database. Copyright 2000 by Biblesoft).

[17] Philippians 2:4.

[18] Acts 1:8. Note the purpose: "You will be my witnesses in Jerusalem, and in all Judea and Samaria, and to the ends of the earthyou shall be witnesses to Me in Jerusalem, and in all Judea and Samaria, and to the end of the earth."

[19] *Shekinah* (she-ki'-na) (*shekhinah*, "that which dwells," from the verb *shakhen*, or *shakhan*, "to dwell," "reside"): This word is not found in the Bible, but there are allusions to it in Isaiah 60:2; Matthew 17:5; Luke 2:9, where it describes the glory of God manifested as powerful brightness. (from the *International Standard Bible Encyclopaedia*, Electronic Database Copyright 1996 by Biblesoft).

[20] Acts 2:5-11.

[21] Acts 2:9-11.

[22] 1 Corinthians 14:24-25.

[23] Ephesians 1:5.

[24] John 16:8.

[25] John 16:13.

[26] John 16:14-15.

[27] Ephesians 1:20; 2:6.

[28] 1 Corinthians 12:27; Ephesians 1:22, 23; 2:22.
[29] Ephesians 3:10.
[30] Matthew 16:16.
[31] Matthew 16:17.
[32] Matthew 16:18.

Chapter Two

[1] W. A. Beckham may be reached at wabeckham@aol.com. His written works are available through the publisher's web site, www.touchusa.org.
[2] Luke 18:18-30.
[3] Acts 20:24, *NKJV.*
[4] Thomas Kuhn, Thomas, *The Structure of Scientific Revolutions* (Chicago: The University of Chicago Press, 1966), 90.

Chapter Three

[1] http://www.ag.org/enrichmentjournal/199904/026_azusa.cfm.
[2] http://www.christiannet.co.za/revival/jglake.htm.
[3] Verbal report from many Apostolic Faith pastors as I moved among them in 1996.
[4] http://www.leaderu.com/isot/docs/3wave.html.
[5] Throughout this book, we will treat the Greek word *ekklesia* by using the term *community* instead of "church," a word that connects in the modern mind to a physical structure, rather than the literal meaning, "called out people." When the term "church" is used in this book, it is selected to define a religious building where Christians gather for formal meetings. Interestingly, this term was substituted for "church" early in the last century by Adolf Schlatter, theologian in the faculty of Protestant Theology at Tubingen, Germany (1852-1938). Dr. Andreas Köstenberger, translator of Schlatter's books, explains: "Schlatter defined *ekklesia* as *community* and hence avoided to use the term 'church' (in the original German, the distinction is between *Kirche* [church] and *Gemeinde* [community], and Schlatter consistently uses the latter rather than the former").
[6] Bartleman, Frank, *Another Wave of Revival* (Springdale, PA: Whitaker House, 1962), 95-96.
[7] John 7:38.
[8] We must always frame such statements by realizing that we cannot separate the Godhead into "compartments." The Holy Spirit, the Spirit of Christ, and so forth are synonymous. The error is made when compartmentalization takes place.
[9] For more information about the study, visit www.barna.org.
[10] Address given May 2, 2005, at the Cathedral of the Pines, Beaumont, Texas.
[11] William A. Beckham, *The Second Reformation* (Houston: Touch Publications, 1997), 25.
[12] Email sent 10/22/2005. karenhurston@cs.com
[13] "For in Christ all the fullness of the Deity lives in bodily form, and you have been given fullness in Christ, who is the head over every power and authority" For in Him dwells all the fullness of the Godhead bodily; and you are complete in Him, who is the head of all principality and power.*(NKJV).*
[14] Burgess and McGee, editors, *Dictionary of Pentecostal and Charismatic Movements* (Grand Rapids, Michigan: Zondervan Publishing House), 96.
[15] http://www.apologeticsindex.org/b05.html.
[16] William Branham, *Footprints on the Sands of Time: The autobiography of William Marrion Branham, Part Two* (Jeffersonville, IN: Spoken Word Publications, 1975), 606-7.
[17] S. David Moore, "William J. Seymour," *Ministries Today*, May/June 2005, 48.

Chapter Four

[1] Cho, David Yonggi, *Successful Home Cell Groups* (Bridge-Logos Publishers, 1981, reprinted 2001).
[2] 1 Corinthians 14:24, 25.
[3] *Ecclesiology* is the theological term used to define the nature and scope of the church. The Greek word for "church" is *ekklesia.*

[4] Revelation 2:4.

[5] 1 Corinthians 11:22.

[6] Robert Banks, Robert: *Paul's Idea of Community* (Peabody, Massachusetts, 1994), 38-41.

[7] From *The Message: The Bible in Contemporary Language* © 2002 by Eugene H. Peterson (my emphasis).

[8] Ibid.

[9] Banks, *op. cit.*, 27.

[10] *Ibid.*, p. 31.

[11] Frank Viola, Frank, *God's Ultimate Passion* (Gainesville, FL: Present Testimony Ministry, 2006), 15.

[12] From *The Message: The Bible in Contemporary Language* © 2002 by Eugene H. Peterson.

[13] Ibid.

[14] John 4:32.

[15] The informal name of the West Memorial Baptist Church, Dairy Ashford Road, Houston.

[16] Cal Thomas and I co-authored a book about all this: *Target Group Evangelism* published by Broadman Press in 1975.

[17] For further information, see these web sites: www.touchusa.org; www.touchglocal.com; an example of one such target group on line is www.liftgroups.com.

[18] New King James Version.

[19] Romans 8:26.

[20] "There Shall Be Showers Of Blessing," Words by Daniel W. Whittle, 1883.

[21] Revelation 22:17.

[22] John 1:12.

[23] Revelation 22:17 (my emphasis).

[24] Revelation 22:16-17.

[25] http://www.cornerstonenet.org

[26] See http://www.barna.org.

[27] Some have challenged that figure. Lumpkin did an extensive survey over three years of the over more than 3,700 churches in Greater Houston, using dozens of volunteer students. They computed the approximate total number of seats in all the auditoriums, the average attendances per week of people who filled those pews. By the most lenient total, they documented that less than 12% percent of Houstonians darken the doors of the Protestant, Evangelical, and Catholic churches of the city. In 2005, the population was 2,086,582 souls. This means that 250,390 people attend one or more services a month. Further, the large megachurches are growing by absorbing members from smaller congregations. There are some realtors who specialize in selling church properties in the "Bible Belt!"

Chapter Five

[1] Thomas G. Bandy, *Christian Chaos*, (Nashville, TN: Abingdon Press, 1999), 318.

[2] Second Baptist Church in Houston, Texas, accepted into membership a congregation that voted to merge into the larger structure, even though they possessed millions of dollars of property and over more than 1,500 members. This provided a third campus for the second largest church in the metropolis.

[3] In Northwest Houston, a chapel belonging to the Southern Baptists was bought by a real estate developer and resold to a local group of investors who turned it into a Hare Krishna temple.

[4] Matthew 18:20.

[5] Philippians 2:5 (*NKJV*).

[6] Philippians 2:12, 13.

[7] Jerome Murphy-O' Connor, *St. Paul's Corinth, Texts and Archaeology* (Wilmington, DE: Glazier, 1983), 155.

[8] Vincent Branick, *The House Church in the Writings of Paul* (Wilmington, DE: Glazier, 1989), 41-42.

[9] 1 Peter 5:14.

[10] Ephesians 2:19.

[11] 1 Corinthians 12:25-27.

[12] Robert Banks, *Paul's Idea of Community* (Peabody, Massachusetts: Hendrickson Publishers, Inc.,1994), 82-83.

[13] Hebrews 10:24-25.

Chapter Six

[1] Volume 1, Jan/Feb 2002 #7 p. 1.

[2] Michael J. Papesh, *Clerical Culture: Contradiction and Transformation* (Collegeville, MN: Liturgical Press, 2004), 36.

[3] William A. Beckham, William A., *The Second Reformation* (Houston: Touch Publications, 1997).

[4] http://www.zinzendorf.com/countz.htm.

[5] See Psalms 22:25; 35:18; 40:9, 10.

[6] http://www.nihn.org.

[7] http:// www.churchunderthebridge.org.www.churchunderthebridge.org/

[8] http://www.missionwaco.org.

[9] Paul Tournier, Paul, *A Place For You.* (New York: Harper and Row, 1968), 10.

[10] Ibid, 40.

[11] 1 Corinthians 3:16, 17.

[12] 2 Corinthians 6:16.

[13] Ephesians 2:21, 22.

Chapter Seven

[1] To define our fallen nature, we simply remove the vowel from the consonants in the word "sIn." The "I" is that independent spirit of man that says, "I, myself, am like God."

[2] In speaking of the Trinity, the term *identity* refers to centers of relationship.

[3] See also 2 Corinthians 13:14; Hebrews 9:14.

[4] John 3:16; Matthew 3:17.

[5] John 14:26.

[6] Jürgen Moltmann, *The Trinity and the Kingdom* (San Francisco: Harper and Row, 1981), 169.

[7] Colossians 2:910, *NKJV.*

[8] John 14:9.

[9] John 14:26, 27, *NKJV.*

[10] From Jamieson, Fausset, and Brown Commentary, Electronic Database. Copyright 1997 by Biblesoft. Cf also John 16:12-15.

[11] Romans 8:26, 27.

[12] Mark 9:37, *NKJV.*

[13] John 10:30.

[14] John 1:32.

[15] In an email dated December 2, 2005. See his web site "Reasoning From from Scriptures," http://home.earthlink.net/~ronrhodes./

[16] Revelation 4:8, 15:4.

[17] Revelation 5:9.

[18] Ephesians 1:13, 14.

[19] Adolf Schlatter, *The Theology of the Apostles* (Grand Rapids: Baker Books, 1998), 268.

[20] Matthew 9:38. Note that the harvest does not belong to the workers but to the "Lord of the harvest."

[21] Acts 3:18.

[22] Adolf Schlatter, *Do We Know Jesus?* (Grand Rapids: Kregel Publications, 2005), 37.

[23] Hebrews 10:5-10.

[24] Romans 8:29.

[25] See Matthew 5:16, 45, 48, etc.

[26] 1 Peter 1:3.

[27] Milt Rodriguez, *The Temple Within, Fellowship With an Indwelling Christ* (www.therebuilders.org, 2005), 27-28.

[28] Galatians 4:19.

[29] Matthew 4:23.

[30] John 14:26, 27.

Chapter Eight

[1] 1 Corinthians 15:25.

[2] Daniel 2:44, 45.

[3] See also Luke 8:1 for the expansion of His his activity; the assignment to the disciples is given in Luke 9:2.

[4] Matthew 13:11, *NKJV*. Because of the sacredness of the word *God*, in Matthew substituted the term *heaven* is substituted for *God*. There is only one kingdom, not two.

[5] Matthew 4:8.

[6] Revelation 11:15.

[7] Matthew 13:33.

[8] Mark 1:14, *NKJV*.

[9] Matthew 11:4-6.

[10] Matthew 10:7-10.

[11] E. Stanley Jones, E. Stanley, *The Unshakable Kingdom and the Unchanging Person* (Bellingham, Washington: McNett Press, 1972), 289-291.

[12] Manfred Haller, *The Mystery of God, Christ All in All*, http://therebuilders.org; The Rebuilders, p. 43.

[13] 1 Corinthians 14:24. *Prophesying* here refers to any manifestation Christ provides in the *ekklesia* to edify other body members. This will be further explained in the chapter on the gifts of Christ.

[14] 1 Corinthians 14:24, 25.

[15] Words: John Newton; Music: Edwin O. Excell, 1917.

[16] Matthew 17:121-13.

[17] Luke 22:44.

[18] Philippians 2:4.

[19] Genesis 4:4.

[20] Isaiah 53.

[21] John 1:29.

[22] 1 Peter 2:8, *NKJV*.

[23] From *O Timothy Magazine*, Volume 12, Issue 7, 1995. David W. Cloud, Editor, www.wayoflife.org.

[24] Galatians 2:20.

[25] *Ekklesia*.

[26] Galatians 3:28, 29.

[27] Touch Family in Houston, Texas, has a blend of 9 nine nationalities so far in a city with over more than 170. We seek to live by the motto, "A church of the nations for the nations."

[28] See *Matthew Henry's Commentary on the Whole Bible: New Modern Edition*, Electronic Database. Copyright 1991 by Hendrickson Publishers, Inc.

[29] Luke 4:18, 19.

[30] Cf. Leviticus 25:13. Every 50th year was to be announced as a jubilee year. All real property should automatically revert to its original owner (25:10; compare verse 13), and those who, compelled by poverty, had sold themselves as slaves to their brothers, should regain their liberty (25:10; compare verse 39). (from International Standard Bible Encyclopaedia, Electronic Database Copyright 1996 by Biblesoft)

[31] Todd A. Brown, email dated 4/4/2005.

[32] Mark 10:35-37.

[33] Matthew 20:21, 22.

[34] Mark 9:34.

[35] 2 Timothy 4:7, 8.

[36] 1 Corinthians 3:10 ff.

[37] Ibid.

[38] 1 Corinthians 7:29-31.

Chapter Nine

[1] Leviticus 23:17: *From wherever you live, bring two loaves made of two-tenths of an ephah of fine flour, baked with yeast, as a wave offering of firstfruits to the Lord.*

[2] Cf. Isaiah 60:2; Matthew 17:5; Luke 2:9; Romans 9:4.

[3] Isaiah 6:8-9.

[4] Jeremiah 20:9.

[5] I 1 Peter 2:9, "a people belonging to God." In the Hebrew, *segullah* described a king who chose the finest treasures in the kingdom as his personal property, pronouncing this word over the object.

[6] Matthew 28:20.

[7] 1 Corinthians 12:12, 13.

[8] Colossians 2:9.

[9] 1 Peter 1:1, 2.

[10] Matthew 18:20.

[11] Matthew 14:22.

[12] John 6:26.

[13] Exodus 18:21.

[14] 2 Samuel 24:10.

[15] 1 Corinthians 14:24, 25.

[16] Acts 2:47 and 16:5.

[17] The entire temple occupied 35 acres. It was so split up inside that no large group could assemble. The apostles went there to teach at different times of the day. Evidently the believers clustered in groups small enough that one person's teaching might accommodate 30 or so at one location. See Acts 3:31; 5:20; 5:42 as examples of the various times the apostles taught. There were no set times. There were no mass meetings of thousands taking place in the Temple. They were at best small clusters. Further, teachers in that culture would sit and address a small group, not lecture from a platform.

[18] Acts 2:42-47.

[19] Adolf Schlatter, Adolf, *The Church in the New Testament Period* (London: S.P.C.K., 1961), 29.

[20] 1 Peter 2:4, 5.

[21] Schlatter, ibid, 18.

[22] Schlatter, ibid, 19.

[23] 1 Peter 1:3-5.

[24] Acts 1:7.

[25] 2 Peter 3:10-12.

Chapter Ten

[1] 1 Corinthians 12:13.

[2] Ephesians 1:23.

[3] Gerald Martin is a modern apostle (spelled in lower case!) who ministers to the Cornerstone churches both in America and overseas.

[4] Acts 2:34; 7:35; Hebrews 12:2, and so forth.

[5] Hebrews 2:8.

[6] Ephesians 2:6.

[7] *Now, therefore, you are no longer strangers and foreigners, but fellow citizens with the saints and members of the household of God, having been built on the foundation of the apostles and prophets, Jesus Christ Himself being the chief cornerstone, in whom the whole building, being fitted together, grows into a holy temple in the Lord, in whom you also are being built together for a dwelling place of God in the Spirit (NKJV).*

[8] 1 Corinthians 12:13 (again!).

[9] *Oikodomeo* = edify. Composed of *oikos* = (community) and *domeo* = (to build up).

[10] 2 Corinthians 5:16-21, *NKJV*.

[11] 1 Corinthians 6:15.

[12] I have great love for house churches. I only feel their blindness to the corporate nature of Christ's Basic Body separates them from the task of being "points of light" connected to the rest of the "points."

[13] Ephesians 3:14-19, *NKJV*.

[14] Colossians 3:11.

[15] See Journal *of the Evangelical Theological Society*, June 2000.

[16] See http://www.findarticles.com/p/articles/mi_qa3817/is_200006/ai_n8917127.

[17] George Ladd, George, *A Theology of the New Testament* (Grand Rapids: Wm. B. Eerdmans Publishing Company, 1974), 591.

[18] 1 Corinthians 14:24-, 25. Note that while some translations translate *en* as "among," it is literally "in" or "within." The witness we must bear is not what we do, but what Christ is performing through each and every one of his body members.

Chapter Eleven

[1] Daniel 2:44.

[2] George Eldon Ladd, George Eldon, *The Gospel of the Kingdom* (Grand Rapids: Eerdmans Publishing Company, reprinted in 1981).

[3] http://www.britannia.com/rulebrit.html.

[4] A song by Thomas Augustine Arne, 1740 A.D.

[5] Psalm 103:19.

[6] Psalm 145:10-13.

[7] Matthew 3:2.

[8] Luke 10:9.

[9] Mark 4:11, *NKJV*..

[10] Romans 1:1; Titus 1:1; James 1:1, etc.

[11] Ladd, op. cit., 21.

[12] Ladd, op. cit., 117.

[13] Cf. Luke 10.

[14] Mark 9:19.

[15] Mark 9:28-29.

[16] Ladd, op. cit., 22.-23.

[17] 1 Thessalonians 4:16, 17.

[18] Ladd, op. cit., p. 89.

[19] Hebrews 2:1-4.

Chapter Twelve

[1] 1 Corinthians 12:27.

[2] Galatians 2:20.

[3] 1 Corinthians 12:12, 13.

[4] N. T. Wright, N. T., *Paul*. (Minneapolis, MN: Fortress Press, 2005), 164-165.

[5] Romans 8:26, 27.

[6] Romans 8:34.

[7] George Barna, George, *Revolution*. (Wheaton, Illinois, Tyndale House Publishers, 2005).

[8] Proverbs 3:6.

[9] Paul Hattaway, *Back to Jerusalem: Three Chinese House Church Leaders Share Their Vision to Complete the Great Commission* (Waynesboro, Georgia: Authentic Media, 2003).

[10] Adolf Schlatter, Adolf, *The Church in the New Testament Period*. (London: S P C K, 1961), 22.

[11] 2 Samuel 6:7.

Chapter Thirteen

[1] John 14:26: *But the Counselor, the Holy Spirit, whom the Father will send in my name, will teach you all things and will remind you of everything I have said to you. But the Helper, the Holy Spirit, whom the Father will send in My name, He will teach you all things, and bring to your remembrance all things that I said to you.*

[2] Romans 8:26.

[3] From *Thayer's Greek Lexicon*, Electronic Database. Copyright © 2000, 2003 by Biblesoft, Inc.

[4] Biblesoft's *New Exhaustive Strong's Numbers and Concordance with Expanded Greek-Hebrew Dictionary.* Copyright © 1994, 2003 Biblesoft, Inc. and International Bible Translators, Inc.

[5] "... *bestow* your luggage where you found it": William Shakespeare, *The Tempest* (1611).

[6] Adolf Schlatter, *Do We Know Jesus?* (Grand Rapids, Kregel Publications, 2005), 57-58.

[7] Matthew 28:18., my emphasis.

[8] Matthew 28:20.

[9] Lesslie Newbigen, Lesslie, *The Open Secret, An Introduction to the Theology of Mission, Revised Edition.* (Grand Rapids, MI: William B. Eerdmans Publishing Company, 1995); 179-180.

[10] Rodriguez, Milt. *The Temple Within, Fellowship With an Indwelling Christ.* (The Rebuilders, http://therebuilders.org, 2005), pp. 27-28.

[11] 1 Thessalonians 5:17, 6-18.

[12] Colossians 1:9-10, *NKJV.*

[13] Corrie Ten Boom and John and Elizabeth Sherrill, *The Hiding Place.* (1971: Old Tappan, NJ, Fleming H. Revell Company).

[14] Milt Rodriguez, Milt, *Ibid.*, p. 123.

[15] Platform comment by Charles Carrin.

Chapter Fourteen

[1] Philippians 2:4.

[2] *Macbeth*, Act 5, scene 5, 19–28.

[3] Adapted from a sermon by Dr. Harold L. White. Email Dr. White at hleewhite@aol.com . His bio: http://www.angelfire.com/fl5/hleewhite/Dr__White_s_Bio_/dr__white_s_bio_.html.

[4] Joel 2:28-32.

[5] Acts 2:18.

[6] Ephesians 4:1411.

[7] Ephesians 4:4-16.

[8] http://jmm.aaa.net.au/articles/8084.htm. Sonscape Creation Ministries is located at 321 East Henrietta Avenue, Woodland Park, CO 80863. (719) 687-7007.

[9] Ephesians 4:12.

[10] Titus 1:5.

Additional Resources by the Author
Available Through TOUCH Publications

PASTORAL LEVEL

Where Do We Go From Here? A Guidebook for the Cell Group Church

The Navigation Guide for Making Cell Groups Work (contributor)

GROUP LEADER LEVEL

The Shepherd's Guidebook: Spiritual and Practical Foundations for Cell Group Leaders

MEMBER LEVEL

Welcome To Your Changed Life

The Journey Guides for New Christians and Growing Christians

Beginning the Journey

The Arrival Kit

Mentoring Another Christian

The Touching Hearts Guidebook

The Opening Hearts Trilogy

Call 1-800-735-5865 *for a catalog of Dr. Neighbour's resources or visit our web site at www.touchusa.org*

First-Time Buyer's Coupon

Have you read the book that stirred the church world? Where Do We Go From Here? provides a complete explanation of how a cell-based church operates and provides a solid theological foundation as well. If you have not read this classic, order it today and save $10 off the retail price of $21.50 ($11.50 + S/H)

Offer good for one copy of this title for new customers through TOUCH Publications. Call to place your order today and mention "CBB coupon" when ordering. Offer not valid through web site orders, and cannot be used for quantity purchases or other titles or refunded or credited after the purchase. **1-800-735-5865**

Printed in the United States of America
by Publisher's Express Press, Ladysmith, Wisconsin